T0209623

PREVIOUS BOOKS

Spiritual Wisdom for Peace on Earth From Sananda
Channeled through David J Adams

LOVE is the **KEY.** Part 1
Spiritual Wisdom from Germain
Channeled through David J Adams

LOVE is the **KEY.** Part 2
Spiritual Wisdom from Germain
Channeled through David J Adams

WE ARE ALL ONE
Spiritual Wisdom from The Masters of Shambhala
Channeled through David J Adams

ENLIGHTENMENT AND ILLUMINATION
Spiritual Wisdom from Djwahl Khul
Channeled through David J Adams

COSMIC SYMPHONY OF LOVE
Spiritual Wisdom from Hilarion
Channeled through David J Adams

THE NEW EARTH
Spiritual Wisdom from The Merlin, Ar'Ak and Spirit of
Crystals and Gemstones
Channeled through David J Adams

GATEWAY OF LOVE

Spiritual Wisdom from
TARAK, DYLANTHIA, MARGOT, NEPTUNE

DAVID J ADAMS

authorHOUSE

AuthorHouse™
1663 Liberty Drive
Bloomington, IN 47403
www.authorhouse.com
Phone: 1 (800) 839-8640

Published by AuthorHouse 10/24/2019

ISBN: 978-1-7283-3328-1 (sc)
ISBN: 978-1-7283-3326-7 (hc)
ISBN: 978-1-7283-3327-4 (e)

Library of Congress Control Number: 2019917310

Print information available on the last page.

Any people depicted in stock imagery provided by Getty Images are models, and such images are being used for illustrative purposes only. Certain stock imagery © Getty Images.

The Front Cover Sacred Geometry is called the "The Diamond Labyrinth of Transcendence". It has been painted and photographed by Kaye Ogilvie, Intuitive artist from Queensland, Australia.

Back cover Photo was taken on the camera of David J Adams, the T shirt was created by Tie Dye artist, Ruth Cary Cooper from USA.

This book is printed on acid-free paper.

DEDICATION

I Dedicate this book to my children, Nicky and Suzi, my grandchildren, Lauren, Matthew and Emily, and my great grandchildren, Ruby–Rae and Peyton, for they and others of the next generations will carry the Light forward and create the Peace that we all yearn for.

ABOUT THE AUTHOR

ADAMS, David John Patrick

Born: 28th April 1943

At: Mountain Ash, Glamorgan, South Wales, UK.

Moved to South Australia in 1971, Currently living in the southern suburbs of the city of Adelaide.

Began his Spiritual Journey as a result of the Harmonic Convergence in late 1987.

In 1991, he was asked by Beloved Master Germain to undertake a global Meditation based on, and working with, the Consciousness of the Oceans, which was called the Marine Meditation.

In 2009 he was asked to address a Peace Conference in Istanbul to speak of the Marine Meditation and his work for World Peace through meditation.

He is a Songwriter, a Musician, an Author and Channel, but most of all a **SERVANT OF PEACE**.

David began bringing through information from a variety of Masters and Cosmic Beings in the form of Meditations around 1991. It was not, however, until after the year 2000 that he began to channel messages in group situations and in individual sessions. Most of these messages were not recorded or transcribed so remain shared with only a few people, but in 2009 the messages being brought through in the weekly Pendragon Meditation group began to be recorded and transcribed by Kath Smith and sent out around the world on David's own Pendragon network.

David's special Guide and Mentor has been 'The Germain, the I am that I am', but he has also worked extensively with – and channeled - Sananda, Hilarion, Djwahl Khul, AA Michael, The Merlin, The Masters of Shambhala, as well as Arcturian Sound Master Tarak and his own Home Trinity Cosmic Brother Ar'Ak.

(Contact email – <u>djpadams8@tpg.com.au</u>)

ACKNOWLEDGEMENTS

I, David J Adams, would like to acknowledge three special Earth Angels.

Heather Niland/Shekina Shar - who helped me to awaken to my Journey in 1987 and connected me to my Beloved Friend "The Germain", she was a mentor, guide and teacher way ahead of her time.

Meredith Pope – who walked in the same shoes as me in those difficult early years as a fellow 'weekender' at The EarthMother Centre, and was - and still is - an inspiration to me.

Krista Sonnen – An Harmonic and Earthwalker, who helped to build the bridges to my Spiritual and Cosmic friends by persistently urging me to allow them to speak through me in private sessions, then in group sessions. Without her support these messages would not be here.

I would further like to acknowledge **Kath Smith** – A spiritual Being of immense Love and Joy who initiated the recording and transcribing of the messages received in Pendragon so that the messages from our 'other Dimensional friends' would not be lost forever. Also **Takara Shelor,** who combined her Global Water Dolphin Meditation with the Marine Meditation in 1998 and has organized the Marine Meditation website as an adjunct to her own Dolphin Empowerment website ever since. Also **Kaye Ogilvie**, Intuitive Spiritual Artist, who Painted all the Labyrinths walked during the Marine Meditations, as well as many other inspirational images that have assisted my Journey of Growth.

I also acknowledge all those here in Australia and those throughout the World who have supported me and encouraged me over the years, and in particular**, Barbara Wolf and Margaret Anderson**, who's vision and hard work has made this book possible.

BLESSINGS OF LOVE, JOY AND PEACE TO EACH AND EVERY ONE OF YOU.

DAVID J ADAMS

FOREWORD

The whole of the Universe is comprised of Sound Vibrations and Sound Frequencies, in fact there is really no such thing as real silence. We may only be aware of Sound through what we hear in our Human ears, but the reality is that Sound Frequencies go way beyond the Human capacity to hear, *Sound reverberates through every atom of our Being.* The messages within this book deal with Sound Vibrations and Frequencies on a Cosmic level as well as an Earthly level, as those giving the messages are all *Masters of Sound* in one form or another, and I hope they will provide you with inspiration and upliftment, and Wisdom you did not have before. Just remember, smile, *Discernment at all times !*

We Humans live in the concept of "Linear Time', which divides 'Time' into minutes, hours, days, months, etc. and goes in a straight line from 'Past' through 'Present' to 'Future', consequently we give importance to the date on which something happens. Our Spiritual and Cosmic Friends are not bound by such constraints, they operate in the **'Now'** moment, so although the messages within this book have 'dates' attached to them, they are, essentially, **TIMELESS**.

Some messages do, of course, refer to specific events, such as the Equinox or the Solstice, or even some man made event, however, the underlying message is always **TIMELESS**. So we ask, when you read these messages, that you accept them as having importance within the **'Now Moment'** of your lives. Although we have given the date of receipt at the end of each message, they are not in sequential 'linear time' order.

All messages were received within the Pendragon Meditation Circle and always began with the 'Sounding" of the Tibetan Bowls, the Blessings Chimes, the Drum, and occasionally other percussion instruments. Many of the messages make reference to these Sound frequencies.

Let the messages speak to your Heart, for that is what they were intended to do when they were given by **Tarak, Dylanthia, Margot and Neptune**.

Blessings of Love, Peace and Joy

David J Adams

INTRODUCTION

Tarak is a Sound Master of Arcturus, and travels the Cosmos to work with 'Sound' Vibrational frequencies on various Planetary Systems. He comes to the Earth Planet whenever requested to do so by Earth Mother and works primarily through the 12 major Songlines. He first connected with us when we were drawn to the Sacred Space at Willow Springs and tapped in to the '*Rivers of Energy*' that form the confluence of the Michael and Mary lines there. He works with us from within the Pyramid of Sound at Willow Springs.

He has worked with us as part of the Marine Meditation since around 1999, as the Whales and the Dolphins are powerful 'Sounders' of the Ocean, he has also worked with us on the Songlines as well as the Crystalline Grid system of the Earth. We have been so grateful to have received the benefit of his Cosmic Wisdom and we hope that you, too, will benefit from those portions that we are able to present to you within this book.

Dylanthia is a Being from Sirius that can best be described as a 'Sound Engineer'. She and her sister Arantha are responsible for balancing and aligning the energies of the 12 major Songlines, she at Sundown Hill near Broken Hill in New South Wales, Australia and her sister Arantha at Machu Picchu, these are the two meeting points on the Earth Planet of the 12 Songlines. From the time of the very beginning of the Planet members of **Dylanthia's** race (Sirians) have been placed upon the Earth to assist with the maintenance of the Songlines, which are Cosmic Strands of Light, and **Light resonates as Sound.**

Dylanthia connected with us when our Sounder, the Harmonic and Earth Walker **Krista Sonnen** was called to visit the 12 Sculptures on Sundown Hill in 2004 to act as a 'tuning fork' to recalibrate the Songlines that had been corrupted as a result of mining activities in the area. We were given information in sessions between Krista and myself that the Sculptures marked each Songline, so we have worked on this basis ever since. At one point **Dylanthia** left Sundown Hill to be 'upgraded' into the new Dimensional Frequencies of the Earth, but returned a year later to resume her duties there. **SUNDOWN HILL** is of immense importance, but of course it is little known as a Sacred Space. We hope many will awaken to its significance in the future.

Master Sounder Margot was first known to me as Margot Wilson when in 1996 she came to my Spirit of Crystals Centre to run some 'Sounding' workshops. She quickly became an integral part of our Marine Meditations with her amazing Sounding, and then we shared time in various groups that either she ran or I ran.

Margot Wilson passed into Spirit in 2012 and almost immediately I received a message from her in Spirit to say that she had been invited to work in the Library of Arcturus as part of a Cosmic 'Sound' team led by **Tarak**.

I received some information from her over the next period of time but it wasn't until September of 2015 that she was finally of sufficient Light Frequency to effect a ***magnetic interface*** with me and channel through me. It was then that she revealed herself as a Master Sounder, and she explains that in one of her messages within this book. She and *Tarak* have been regular visitors to the Sound Pyramid at Willow Springs since that time and we have done much 'Sound' work together in Pendragon and around the World. I hope you will find her contribution to this book inspiring, although I'm sure she would prefer if you could hear her rather than just read her words, but then, smile, if you close your eyes after reading and just listen with your Heart, I am sure that she will 'Sound' for you with great Joy.

Neptune – Has been known for eons of time by Humanity as the God of the Sea and was often Portrayed by the Romans riding in a Chariot pulled by Sea creatures. Those perceived as Gods by both the Romans and the Greeks in ancient times were in reality time lords or Cosmic Beings of Light who periodically made themselves known to impart wisdom or assist the Earth Planet in its ascension process.

Neptune first connected with me in 1991 when I was asked to begin the twice yearly Marine Meditations at the March and September Equinoxes, and worked closely with Beloved Germain, then with Germain, Hilarion and Djwahl Khul, as the Meditations have continued, He often channeled through me in the lead up to the Marine Meditation celebrations, and those of his messages that were recorded are included as part of this book. It needs to be remembered that two thirds of the Earth Planet is covered by Oceans, so 'Sounders' within the Oceans such as Whales and Dolphins have been and continue to be of paramount importance in holding the Earth in balance and enabling the Ascension of the Earth to progress.

I hope you will embrace **Neptune's** contribution with Love in your Hearts.

Blessings of Love, Peace and Joy to all four contributors.

David J Adams
(djadams8@tpg.com.au)

CONTENTS

1

MAGENTA LIGHT OF LOVE AND PEACE

(The Circle opens with the Blessings Chimes, the Tibetan Bowl and the Drums)

Allow yourselves to become totally immersed in *'Sound'*, allowing the different resonances to seep into the very Heart of your Being, for it is the Heart that is the creative essence of all things. All Light stems from within the Heart, all Sound resonates from within the Heart, all colour evolves from seeds of Light within the Heart, so focus on your Heart, not just your physical Heart, your Soul Heart, the deepest and highest Heart within your Multidimensional Being. Although you perceive these Hearts as being separate within your three dimensional imagery, they are of course *All One*, and everything emanates from within your Heart.

Greetings Dear Hearts, I am Tarak - Sound Master of Arcturus, and yes Beloved Margot is at my side and we are back to work with you once again in the lead up to your Solstice, to that moment in time, the moment of *'now'* when the Heart of the Earth opens fully and floods the Earth, and the Cosmos beyond the Earth, with the *Magenta Light of Love and Peace.*

We have been asked by Beloved Gaia to be a part of this experience, for as usual Sound Resonance will play a great role in this magnificent *'Awakening of the Heart of the Earth'*, and through the Heart of the Earth the 'Awakening' of the Hearts of all upon the Earth, of all Humanity, of all the creatures of the Earth, all life forms upon the Earth, they will all feel *Magenta Light* washing through them, filling them, and the most appropriate way this can occur is through the Sound Vibrations.

You were told at your gathering last week that it was important to balance the Sound Resonance, to have both the Blessings Chimes and the Drums - the highest frequencies and the Earth frequencies - for the Drum vibrations are very much a part of Mother Earth. Through eons of time it is the Drum that has Sounded and called its messages between Beings upon the Earth, so Beloved Margot and I have come once more to be at the Sound Pyramid at Willow Springs, for as you are well aware, Dear Hearts, Willow Springs and Avalon are connected though the Michael and Mary Confluence energies, so we will work with you here in South Australia at Willow Springs to Sound the Awakening call for the Heart Chakra of Mother Earth at Avalon, and together we will assist Beloved Gaia to open *the Chalice of her Heart* and resonate forth the Magenta energies that will transform the Earth Planet into a Star of great brilliance in the Cosmos.

Since its inception as a Planet, the Earth has been preparing for this moment, there have been opportunities in the past in your linear time for this event to occur, but Humanity itself - as a predominant life form - was not of an appropriate frequency for it to occur. This time, Dear Hearts, Humanity has lifted its Light and its Consciousness to the level necessary for Earth Mother to bloom as a ***Star of Magenta Light in the Cosmos.***

Do you feel the joy within your Heart when you hear that, Dear Ones? the upliftment? this is why you - each one of you - have chosen to be here at this time, not only to participate in it, but to be a ***focal point for it,*** for each one of you has within you the ***Crystal of Divine Peace*** that will be activated by the flow of the Magenta energy from the Heart of Earth Mother. There will be those upon your Planet who will focus their energies, their Sound, their Light, their Love on the Sacred Isle of Avalon, there will be others who will focus upon other Chakras of the Earth, and there will be others - like yourselves - who will focus on Sacred Spaces linked powerfully to the Heart of Mother Earth, in this instance for you, - for all of you here - it is ***Willow Springs.***

Once again, Dear Hearts, this does not necessarily mean you have to be at Willow Springs, but your Hearts have to be connected to Willow Springs, your Heart energies directed with intent through the Michael and Mary confluence at Willow Springs, and the Crystalline structure of the Earth and the Songlines that run through Willow Springs will take that energy to Avalon.

Beloved Merlin, The Lady of the Lake, and The Gate Keeper of Avalon will all be called within their Hearts to be at Avalon for this great occasion, not in physical form, in metaphysical form, for they will take their place in the New Dimensional frequencies that the Chalice Heart will create, where all those who are awakened will see once more the splendour of Avalon where UNITY and ONENESS and EQUALITY were the essence and the theme of life.

It is time for this Unconditional Love to return to the Earth and to be manifested within Humanity.

You may recall, Dear Hearts, that this one, (*David*), was sent to Avalon to return the ***"Consciousness of the Oceans"*** to that Sacred Isle in preparation for what is now to occur. At the time you had no idea why this was necessary, but it is all interlinked, all that you have done over the last 20 years of your Spiritual journeys have been geared to this Cosmic moment of time, the time when Peace flows into the Hearts of every individual. Of course, Dear Hearts, you continue to have free will upon this Planet and there may be those who receive the Magenta energy of Peace but do not accept it, and that is their choice, that is their journey, simply give them Love and focus on the Magenta Peace within your own Hearts and allow that Magenta Peace energy to create the new reality for you. So with your Drums, with your Blessings Chimes, with your Bowls, with your voices, on the day of the Solstice, contribute your resonance to the upliftment of Earth Mother, embrace her with Love as she embraces you with Love.

Beloved Margot and I will be with you on that day, within your Hearts - should you invite us to be within your Hearts - and *we will Sound together the new chapter of Life for the Earth Planet.*

Blessings Dear Hearts.

(1ST June 2015)

2

WAVE OF SOUND FREQUENCIES

(The Circle opens with the Sounds of the Tibetan Bowls and the Blessings Chimes)

Allow the Sound Vibrations to soar up into the Heavens, lifting you into your Soul Dimension, lighting the deepest recesses of your Heart with a Melody of Light, and a Melody of Sound.

Greetings Dear Hearts, I am Tarak, Sound Master of Arcturus,

I come tonight with your beloved friend The Master Sounder Margot to share the Love and the Light of this Circle, and to feel the embrace of your Hearts. We are so deeply honoured to be within this Circle to feel the Love that radiates forth across the Earth.

Dear Hearts, for many of your Earth years you have worked powerfully with the special energies of the Equinox, and through those special energies you have connected your Hearts and your Souls to the Consciousness of the Oceans of your Planet - and those within the Oceans of the Planet that have been contributing to the Ascension of the Earth and all upon it.

It has therefore been decided that there will be a special inflow of *'Sound Vibrational Frequencies'* from the Library of Arcturus at the time of the upcoming Equinox, and we are here tonight to invite you, and through you to invite all the *'Sounders'* of the Earth to come together on the day of the Equinox to open your Hearts and embrace a New Vibration of Sound that infuses the whole of the Earth Planet - but particularly the Oceans of your Planet. For this Ray of Sound is designed specifically to activate the *'Sounders of the Oceans', the Whales and the Dolphins,* to open a Gateway of their Souls, to lift their Songs into a New Vibrational Frequency that will stabilize the Earth in a higher frequency again from what it is now.

You see Dear Hearts, as well you know, *Sound is what creates change, Vibrational Frequencies create change,* and all the work that you have done together with the Whales and the Dolphins over many of your Earth years are now coming to a fulfilment.

Through the work that you have done with the Songlines of the Earth, you have opened Gateways to your own Souls. It is now time to open the gateways to the *Soul of the Whales and the Dolphins*, that they too may lift their Vibrational Frequencies, and through their Songs communicate to all the creatures of the Ocean the New Earth Frequencies, that

ALL may be uplifted and ALL may be awakened within the Oceans of the world.

Although primarily this ***Wave of Sound Frequencies*** is destined for the Whales and the Dolphins, because you are now in a Dimension of Oneness, you too will be impacted by these New Sound Frequencies.

We therefore invite you to gather, to open your Hearts, to be beside the Oceans, and as you feel the flow of Sound Frequencies resonating deep within your Hearts, we ask you to Sound those Vibrations powerfully to the Oceans of the Earth - ***speaking of your commitment to the Oneness of all that is.***

Beloved Margot and myself have journeyed from Arcturus once more to work with you through the Sound Temple at Willow Springs, but on that day, which this one tells me is the 22nd of September, we will be standing alongside each and every one of you as you communicate your Love, your commitment with the Whales and the Dolphins. And when you have ***'Sounded your Sound'***, when you have ***'delivered your Love'***, we ask that you go within in silence and stillness, and FEEL the response from the Whales and the Dolphins.

It is a time of great celebration for them, and you are a part of that celebration.

> ***Their Awakening is your Awakening.***
> ***Their Upliftment is your Upliftment.***

The Song Lines of the Earth will carry the New Songs of the Whales and the Dolphins, and will vibrate with the new sense of Joyfulness, of Oneness. A vibration of Divine Love and Peace will flow through the Oceans of the world, and will resonate throughout the Earth itself.

We will not ask you to gather together at the time that you used to gather together at the Equinox, instead we ask you to gather together at the midpoint of your day, and work powerfully with the energies of the Equinox, and ***Become the Oneness***.

Until that time, until that day, we will continue to work quietly with you and through you from the Sound Temple at Willow Springs.

We Bless you, we Love you, we Thank you.

(2nd September 2013)

3

ECSTASY

(The circle opens with the Sounds of the Tibetan Bowls, the shaker and the Blessings Chimes)

Feel the upliftment of Joy within your Hearts, and within this Circle, allowing the energy of Joy to flow from you to touch all other Light Beings upon the Earth. Creating a chorus of Joyful energies all around the Earth. Heart speaking to Heart with the vibration of Sound.

Greetings, Dear Hearts, I am Tarak, Sound Master of Arcturus.

And I thank you for calling me into the circle this evening with your bountiful Joy and your vibrations of Sound. Much has been happening upon Arcturus of late, a new *'Symphony of Light and Love'* is being prepared, to caress Mother Earth, to increase the frequencies of Mother Earth with a new Joyful energy.

Many Beings of Light from many parts of the Cosmos have come together on Arcturus to create this new Symphony of Light and Love and Joy, to assist in the upliftment of the Earth, and this will take place at the Equinox once again, a time when your Hearts connect most powerfully with the Hearts of the Sounders of the Oceans of the Earth, that both Humanity and the Cetacean creatures will come together in deep Love and deep Joy to create a new more powerful Song for the Earth.

It is the next step in the ascension of the Earth Planet. There will be more *'Harmonics'* coming to the Earth at this time, to create a new vibrational Harmony to lift the Earth into a new Dimension of Light. Feel that information resonate deep within your Heart, for this is something that you have been waiting for, that you have been prepared for, for eons of time.

You have already embraced one new Earth Song in recent times, This is the next step forward, the next step upwards, for Mother Earth has called to the Cosmos for this new *Symphony of Sound*. The Sound that takes Joy to a new level of *'Ecstasy'*. It will be a vibrational frequency you have never felt before, although it is a word that you have in your Dictionaries, the word *'Ecstasy'*.

It has often been spoken of in your Religious teachings, the state of *'Ecstasy'*, it is that step beyond *Joy*, and the Earth Planet is now ready to embrace the *State of Ecstasy*. But each and every one of you will need to open your Hearts even wider, even more powerfully, to enable this energy of *'Ecstasy'* to sit comfortably upon and within the Earth Planet.

It is, you might say, a time to move from the quartet into the fully fledged Choir of the Cosmos. And you know, Dear Hearts, when you listen to a full Choir it lifts your Heart, it lifts your Soul, it creates a vibration that fills you and fills the Earth.

Well this, Dear Hearts, is the Choir of the Cosmos, drawn from every Planetary System within the Cosmos, all coming together now to Sing the Song of the Earth. The Song of the Ascended Earth, *The Song of Ecstasy.*

Take some time between now and the Equinox to commune with your Brothers and Sisters in the Oceans of the Earth, to reach out your Love, and receive the Love from them, so that when the time comes you will lift your voices together in Oneness, in Unity, in Harmony, and you will lift the Earth into its true place in the Cosmos, into its true reality.

AND THAT REALITY, DEAR HEARTS, IS ECSTASY.

(4th August 2014)

4

RIVERS OF ENERGY

(The Circle opens with the Sounds of the Tibetan bowls and the Blessings Chimes.)

Feel the resonance of the Tibetan bowls and the Blessings Chimes moving you ever deeper into the embrace of Earth Mother's Heart, and feel the Divine unconditional Love of Earth Mother wrap around you and flow through you and become the *Oneness*. Feel your physical vessel becoming Lighter and Lighter and Lighter, releasing any dark shadows of fear that remain from your temporary visit to the third Dimensional illusion, and feel yourself becoming the Light and the Love of *all*. Feel the Sound of Love move through every pore of your body, every cell of your body and allow yourselves to float in the 'Ocean of Love'.

Greetings, Dear Hearts, I am Tarak, Sound Master of Arcturus.

I am delighted to be with you this evening from your Sacred Space at Willow Springs, for there is so much happening upon and within the Earth Planet at this time, so many new energies flowing into the Earth and being embraced by Earth Mother, but this is just the beginning of a flow of energy so immense and so intense that you need to be aware that it is about to happen, to prepare your physical vessels, to prepare your Souls to be the natural receptors of this energy, to share with Earth Mother the enlightenment that will occur as a result of these energies flowing to you from different parts of the Cosmos, but also from the very Heart of your own Earth Planet.

As I have said, we are coming to you tonight from your Sacred Space at Willow Springs. The beginning of your awareness of this Sacred place was the energies of the confluence of what you refer to as the Michael and Mary Lines, these are very particular *'rivers of energy'*. You have always been told that they were *'rivers of energy'*, not Ley lines, not Sound lines, not Songlines, but *'rivers of energy'* and at Willow Springs there is a confluence of two *'rivers of energy'*, complementary energy flows coming together in the embrace of Love.

You are also being told that this happening of confluence of energies also occurs on the Isle of Avalon that you are also connected to. These are of course not the only confluences of these two energy lines, these *'rivers of energy'* lines across the Earth, but for you here they are the two of greatest significance - but no one has yet enlightened you as to what these confluences of energy represent, so tonight I wish to advise you that these are, within the Earth, what you and your scientists perceive in the Cosmos as Gateways to other Dimensional Frequencies, *'wormholes'* I believe you have popularly called them, the confluence of energies coming together to create a Gateway.

Willow Springs and Avalon are Gateways at opposite sides of the Earth, but they lead to the same Dimensions within the Earth, for as you have also been told *the Earth is a Multidimensional Being in its own right,* and by working with these particular areas you are able to access different Dimensions of the Earth Planet. You are no longer merely on the surface of the Earth Planet, you can move through these Gateways deep into the Dimensional Frequencies of Earth Mother, and over this next period of time leading up to your Solstice these Gateways to the inner Dimensions of the Earth Planet will be opening, and will remain open, for a considerable period of time and you are being invited to move your Consciousness into these Gateways, into these *'wormholes'* and explore more of the Being that you call Earth Mother.

It is an opportunity to further experience your *Oneness* with the Earth. *It will not be a physical journey, it will be a journey of Consciousness, an awakening within your Heart that allows you to traverse the multidimensionality of your Planet* for you to gain a greater understanding of what being One with the Earth means for you.

You have been made aware over recent times that previous Beings upon the Earth Planet have placed themselves in hibernation awaiting the vibrational frequency of the Earth to rise to a level where they can awaken, just as you are awakening - the pods from Lemuria, Atlantis and many other ancient civilizations are all opening, and the reason they are opening, Dear Hearts, is not only to assist

Humanity to further increase the level of Light upon the Earth Planet, but it is to enable THEM also to explore the Multidimensionality of the Earth Planet.

These are amazing times upon the Earth. Earth Mother is coming into full bloom and is opening her Heart to every Being of Light upon and within. Can you feel the resonance of that within your Hearts, Dear Ones? Beloved Margot and I have asked to remain at Willow Springs to participate in this awakening - for the opening of the Gateways - that we too may participate in the inter-dimensional journey to the Heart of Earth Mother, where our Sound will assist in the stabilization of these *'wormholes'*, that they may be accessible to all who are awakened enough at this time to simply open their Hearts and traverse the Dimensions of the Earth.

Allow yourselves to feel the trembling of the Dimensional Veils as they begin to weaken and fall away. Allow yourselves to focus between now and the Solstice on YOUR confluence of energies, draw it into your Heart and give yourselves permission to journey into the full Oneness of beloved Earth and the full Oneness of your own Being.

All over the Earth Planet these confluences of energy will come alive, will be open and inviting - go with the flow, let Love guide you into the embrace of ALL THAT IS.

(6ᵗʰ June 2016)

5

'SOUND' RELEASES ALL THAT IS NOT IN HARMONY WITH DIVINE LOVE.

(The Circle opens with the Sounds of the Tibetan bowls, the message sticks and the 'Cosmic Tone')

Feel yourselves being uplifted by the resonance of Sound, opening your Heart, freeing your Soul to embrace the Earth Planet with the vibrational frequency of Divine Love. Feel the power within yourself, the power of Love, and radiate forth that Love to all upon and within the Earth Planet, for as each Heart is opened and uplifted the Earth Planet itself is opened and uplifted into its own Soul Dimension.

Greetings Dear Hearts, I am Tarak, Sound Master of Arcturus, and, of course, I am accompanied as usual by Beloved Margot who embraces each and every one of you within this Circle with the Divine Love that has always been within her Heart - and so openly shared with each and every one of you during her time on your Planet.

We come together to embrace you with our Sound, the Sound of Love, the Sound of Joy and the Sound of Freedom. Yes Dear Hearts, we are aware of Beloved Hilarion's message of Freedom, and we come to add to that message, to engage you in Sound Frequencies that help to release you from the enslavements of the past, from the imprisonment of yourself in your own ancient belief systems.

'Sound' is a vibration that shakes and shudders through your very Being, and releases all that is not in Harmony with Divine Love. As you hear and feel the vibration of the Tibetan bowl or the sticks, feel the old energies shifting away, loosening within you and being released, that your physical vessel and your energy vessel is filled with the Harmonious Sound of Divine Love.

As you come towards your special time of the Equinox, we ask you to focus the Sound within your Heart on those areas of your Planet that are currently in darkness. Reach out with the Sound of your Heart to all those on your Planet in pain at this time, those that feel lost and alone.

Your Sound of Love, your Vibration of Love will uplift them, for each one needs to lift their face to the Stars and embrace the Universal energy of Love, and in so doing they will be Enlightened, and a new spark of Joy will begin within them, and as they then look around them, look at the world around them, they will begin to see the Enlightenment of Spirit, and that Enlightenment of Spirit will flow back into them and uplift them even more.

Ascension and Enlightenment is within the grasp of each and every Being on the Earth Planet, it requires only the will to embrace it, and that will comes from self-Love.

It is so important Dear Hearts to embrace yourselves, and to find that spark of Light within yourselves and allow it – no, COMMAND IT - to grow within you, and as Joy begins to filter through you, it begins to show in your external Being, and it begins to touch all those around you, giving each of them the opportunity to find that spark within themselves.

You have spoken tonight of healing and it is indeed that you cannot command the healing in anyone else, you can only provide the spark which they must choose to embrace.

Sound is a great healing energy, but only when you accept it into your Heart.

We will be with you on your Equinox, Dear Hearts, we will be together with the whales and the dolphins, and we will be together with you, and we will be singing a song of Love to the Earth and to all the Beings of Light upon the Earth, creating opportunity - opportunity to heal and to grow and to shift in Dimensional Frequency - *if YOU so choose !*

We will, of course, be at the Pyramid of Sound at Willow Springs, and we invite each and every one of you to join us there in Spirit by opening your Hearts to the Sounds of Love that Beloved Margot and I will be creating, as *OUR* gift towards the Ascension of the Earth, and the Ascension of Humanity.

(10th March 2014)

6

SOUND FEEDS YOUR SOUL

(A Tibetan Bowl was Sounded)

I want you to relax, and feel yourself moving into that Sound. Feel yourself becoming that vibration, that Sound. For the whole of the Earth is comprised of Sound Frequencies. The more each of us can become ONE with the Sounds of the Earth, the more we will be at Peace with ourselves.

There are many Sounds within this world that are dis-harmonious to the Human Body. Many of these, of course, are created by Humanity itself, and you know when you hear these particular Sounds that your body reacts adversely, you feel yourself tightening up inside – like when a car screeches around a corner.

Some Sounds created by nature can also be dis – Harmonious to the body. Many react adversely to the Sound of Thunder, even to the Sound of bees or the Sound of certain birds.

Not everything is in Harmony with our own individual bodies. But within our own individual bodies we are each making choices on how we react to the Sounds around us.

The more we can allow ourselves to become One with the Sounds around us, the more we are in Harmony with life itself – in its many forms, natural or man made.

The more we can embrace the Sounds around us, and be at One with those Sounds, the more complete we become.

(The Tibetan Bowl was Sounded again)

So let yourself flow into that Sound, embrace it into the depths of your Heart. Become One with the vibration of that Sound. As you embrace it and become One with that Sound, you begin to feel yourself being uplifted by that Sound.

Someone else may Sound a bowl of a different frequency, a different Sound, and you will once again be invited by that Sound to become One with it.

During the Marine Meditation we were blessed to have the Sound of rain upon the roof. There were some, no doubt, that felt an irritation that their Peace and Serenity was being disturbed by the Sound of the rain on the roof. There were others who literally lifted their Hearts and embraced that Sound, and felt uplifted by it.

The more that you can embrace Sound, and be uplifted by it, the greater the Serenity that comes within your Heart.

Many of you do not realize the degree to which Sound influences your moods, your emotional reactions. You are surrounded by Sound. You may think that at times you are oblivious to the Sounds around you, but you are not. Your body absorbs and embraces ALL of the Sounds, even those Sounds that are not audible to your Earthly ears. They still resonate within your bodies.

So, Sound is an integral part of your Being.

> Feel those words,
> Embrace those words,
> ***Sound is an integral part of your Being !***

The more you seek to block Sound, the more you create the dis – harmony within your physical body, within your emotional body, and even within your Spiritual body.

SOUND FEEDS YOUR SOUL.

I can speak of Sound, for I am **TARAK – Sound Master of Arcturus**, and I can tell you that on every Planet in the Universe, there is Sound. Indeed, every Planet, every Star, is created through Sound, and exists and remains in Balance through Sound.

The Beloved *Harmonics* are responsible for ensuring that each Planet – and particularly your Earth – remains in balance and Harmony. ***They do not do this by blocking Sounds from the Universe. They do this by EMBRACING Sounds from the Universe and Harmonizing them with the structure of the Earth.***

This is a lesson for each of you – not to block the Sounds coming to you from the Universe, and from your World, but to embrace them and seek to harmonize them with the frequencies of your own body.

Every body is different, as you know, so each will need to embrace the Sounds and Harmonize the Sounds individually. Each needs to be aware of the importance of Sound to the wellbeing of your body, to the wellbeing of the Earth itself.

Harmony is the Key

Dis - harmony creates dis – ease within your physical structures of Earth, not only in the Human body but within the Earth itself.

Those areas of the Earth where alterations have taken place which makes dis – harmony, become dis – eased, and you have seen many examples of this throughout your Earth – for example where the Earth is replete with concrete which does not allow the purity of the Sound to be harmonized with the Earth, there are earth movements to a greater degree.

The Earth is continuously re-harmonizing itself – embracing all the Sounds coming to it from the Cosmos and from the many Universes beyond your Cosmos.

It is all about embracing and Harmonizing.

Take just a moment to simply sit and listen to the Sounds around you. It may simply be the Sound of someone breathing, the Sound of someone moving, the Sound of a vehicle in the distance, the Sound of the wind moving outside.

When you find a Sound that disturbs the balance within yourself, do not block it – embrace it.

Re-harmonize your body to be in Oneness with that Sound.

You cannot be One with all that is when you block the Sounds around you.

Sound is not about liking or disliking – it is about embracing and harmonizing - always Harmonizing. Yes, Harmonizing is change, because every moment of every day you are constantly changing.

Your physical hearing changes each moment of each day.
Your reaction to certain Sounds changes in each moment of each day.
For your body, your emotions, your mind and your Spirit are constantly re-harmonizing themselves.

For at all times you are in a state of perfection – and you do not embrace that enough, Dear Ones. You are in a state of perfection, and anything that comes into your life creates challenges and changes.

To remain in your state of perfection your Being has to embrace and Harmonize with ALL that is connected with you.

It is such a simple concept, but it has one premise – and that is your acknowledgement that you are in a state of perfection

Sometimes in your physical Dimension it is difficult to conceive of being in a state of perfection when you have your physical ailments, your dis-harmonies within your body, and your pain. ***But you need to move from focusing upon those to focusing upon the state of perfection that you are.***

The moment you do that, Dear hearts, you will begin the process of harmonizing with all that is around you, and all that is within you.

Self healing has been spoken of many times, but there can be no self healing until you accept, acknowledge and embrace that your natural state is one of Perfection.

(16th April 2011)

7

THE FREQUENCY OF UNICORN

(The circle opens with the Sounds of the Tibetan Bowls, the Blessings Chimes and the Drums)

Greetings, Beloveds, I am **Tarak, Sound Master of Arcturus**, and I greet you with great Love and great Joy. I will begin with a message for each of you tonight in this Circle. I will confirm for you that your Beloved Sister Margot is with us in the Sound Pyramid at Willow Springs at this time. She is in great Light and great Joy, and is bringing to bear her very special *"Earth Love Sound"* to the work that we are doing at this time. She wishes to be remembered to you, and to ask you to connect your Hearts to hers that her *"Earth Love Sound"* may be empowered in the work she has to do.

The work that we are engaged in at this time is most specific. As you are well aware, the Earth has been - how shall we put it? - bombarded by the Illumination Light. Light and Sound are closely aligned, each affects the other. So the inflow of illumined Light to the Earth has changed the resonance of the Earth's structure. This structure essentially is the crystalline grid system of the Earth, and the resonance of the crystalline structure has been increased.

Resonance as you know is the elongated Sound frequencies, not individual Sounds. You may not be aware that all Dimensional Frequencies of the Earth are represented by different resonance frequencies. *As the Illumined Light has flowed into your Planet, and the resonance of the Earth has changed, you are being moved into different Earth Dimensions.* In particular at this time, and in the time between now and what you call your Solstice, *the resonance of the Earth is settling in to the frequency inhabited by Beloved Unicorn.*

As you have been told before, many Beings of Light came to your Planet at the beginning of time with you, to assist in the development of the Earth into its *"Star nature"*. Many of these Beings of Light stepped into other Earth Dimensions for a variety of reasons, but all have continued to work with you, to assist the Earth in its process of Ascension.

The influx of the Illumined Light to your Planet is now lifting the Earth into the Dimensional frequency that beloved Unicorn moved to.

So I am here tonight to ask you to place the Unicorn deeply into your Heart, to bathe it with Love, that the transition of the Earth into the new resonance might be done with great Love - great Harmony, and once again Beloved Unicorn will become a part of your lives – not necessarily in their physical form as you have perceived them over the times, but as part of the *Love frequency*.

As you are aware within this Circle, there is a Unicorn Temple beneath the crystal mountain at Arkaroola, *(Mt Gee),* and we are working with this Temple to enable the resonance to be birthed seamlessly, in this part of the Earth.

There are a number of Crystal Mountains throughout the Planet, and within and beneath each one of these crystal structures lies a Temple of the Unicorn.

Their Sound is needed by the Earth at this time

To work with you

To work with the *'Harmonics'*

To stabilise the Earth in the new resonance frequencies -

The frequencies of Divine Love

The frequencies of Harmony.

We invite you to work with us between now and the Solstice, by focussing your Hearts on the Unicorn Temple at Arkaroola, by Sounding your Love to the Temple beneath the mountain of crystal.

The crystalline grid structure holds the resonance of the Earth. It protects all the other Dimensional Frequencies of the Earth, and it is through the Crystalline Grid that the Light and the Love will flow, and transform the Earth into the new Dimensional Frequency –the frequency that I call *"The frequency of Unicorn"*.

As you move into this new frequency, you will have within your Hearts a greater sense of Oneness, a greater sense of being a part of the whole. The divisions of the past will fade, and you will become more aware within your Heart of your connectivity to all that is, to all Beings upon this Planet - your Oneness - your Harmony.

I ask you now to sit a moment deep within your Heart, and embrace the energies of Beloved Unicorn, to feel the resonance of their Light and their Love within your Heart, and to allow that to flow through you and out into your World - that from one end of the Planet to the other we begin to come together in Oneness. We begin to embrace once more the Divine Light of Beloved Unicorn.

Sit within your Heart. Feel the resonance of Unicorn, and hear the melody of their Love for this Planet, and as you embrace it, begin to Sound it forth, and each day focus your Heart on the Unicorn Temples around the Earth, and Sound your Love - and receive the resonance of Unicorn's Love - *and BE ONE with all that is.*

WE ARE ALL ONE.

And so it is.

(16th April 2012)

8

A CALLING TO ALL BEACONS OF LIGHT ACROSS THE PLANET

(The Tibetan bowls Sound)

Greetings, Dear Hearts, I am Tarak, Sound Master of Arcturus

Allow those waves of Sound to resonate with every cell of your Being, uplifting, recalibrating the very essence of your Being. Allow yourself to become a part of the Sound.

(The Tibetan bowls Sound again)

Feel yourself flow as part of that Sound, out across the Earth, speaking through your Sound to every Being of Light across the Planet - Beings of all forms, of all frequencies, connecting through the waves of Sound – Heart to Heart.

(The Tibetan bowls Sound again, plus the Heart beat rhythm of the Drum)

Allow the beat of your Heart to resonate outwards into the Cosmos, as the beat of a Drum. Feel yourself becoming a part of that vibrational Sound from the Drum, as your Heart becomes the beat of the Drum.

Feel the vibration of the Earth itself become ONE with the beat of the Drum. Feel yourself being uplifted on the frequencies of the rhythm of the Drum.

(The Tibetan bowls Sound again, plus the Heart beat rhythm of the Drum)

The bowls call forth to all the Beacons of Light across the Planet, to come into a oneness of Sound.

(The Tibetan bowls Sound again, plus the Heart beat rhythm of the Drum)

Allow your own Heart Sound to come forth and call upon the Earth itself, to be one with your Heart.

(A Sounding took place)

It is **Sound** that holds the Earth in balance.

It is **Sound** that creates the opportunity for the Earth to Ascend into a new frequency.

At the time of the 11.11.11, a new major shift in the pathway of Ascension will take place upon the Earth. It will be through the Sound frequencies resonating from the Hearts of Enlightened Humanity that will create this major shift of energy.

There are many upon your Earth who are being drawn to Sacred places, to work with the activation again of the

Crystalline Structure of the Earth. This activation will be through Sound.

Many of you here tonight are being drawn again to your Sacred Space at Willow Springs, and I, **Tarak,** will be waiting to share with you the new frequencies of Sound from the Cosmos, that will assist in the activation of Major Crystalline structures of the Earth.

I will not be alone, for there are many Sound Masters that will gather at that time within the Pyramid of Sound. We await you. We are eager to share with you once again.

Let your focus, when you come to this place, be the focus of Sound - the Sound from the purity of your own Hearts. For there will be no room for the Sounds of darkness - only the Sounds of Light.

You will find within you, the Sound frequencies will change, and will uplift you in a very major way.

I look forward to embracing each one of you who comes.

Focus now on the Sounds within your own Heart.

Listen to the beat of your Heart.

The Heart beat rhythm of the Drum Sounds again.

And so it will be.

(17th October 2011)

9

THE GATEWAY OF AWAKENING

(The circle opens with the Sounds of the Tibetan Bowls, the Blessings Chimes and the Drum)

Focus on the 'Self' in the 5th Dimensional frequencies that allows you to identify and experience and observe the 'Self' that is within the lower Dimensional Frequencies, accepting the expansion of your awareness.

Greetings Beloveds, I am Tarak, Sound Master of Arcturus. It has been some time since I came and spoke with you. At the time of your Marine Meditation in September of 2010, in your linear time, you concluded your ceremony by bringing together the Divine Love and the Divine Peace into the Unity of the 5th Dimensional frequencies.

From that very moment you stepped into the 5th Dimensional frequency energies, and you have progressively been embracing more and more of those energies, for those energies are the entrance to the next phase of your journey, your Journey to the Inner Vision of your SELF.

You are already moving forward along the tunnel of Light towards the first gateway of that Journey – *the Gateway of Awakening.* This is not something that will happen in a moment of time at your next Marine Meditation, it is a progression, a movement between Dimensions, and you will witness many examples of Awakening. Awakening of yourself, Awakening of others around you, Awakening of Beings of Light that have been seeded into your world to awaken at the appropriate time.

As you are aware, when I come from Arcturus to your Planet, I work from within the *Pyramid of Sound* at the place you call *Willow Springs*, and already the energies that you commenced with your Marine Meditation have awakened some of the Beings that are needed by the Earth at this time.

They have been awakened by the changes of the Sound Frequencies that the Unity of the Hathors and the Harmonics have created. It is a time of great Joy for these Beings of Light.

It has been explained to you that they were in what you term 'suspended animation' awaiting their awakening, but since in their Dimension and my Dimension there is no linear time, they have simply been waiting for your call. Waiting for you to achieve the correct frequency of Divine Love that is necessary for them to work with you and Beloved Gaia.

Within the Temple of Sound, The Pyramid of Sound at Willow Springs we have taken on board the Unity of the new Sound Frequencies, and have amplified those frequencies – amplified that Sound, worked in Unity with the Songlines, to send these energies coursing through the Earth, *Awakening the Inner Earth, Awakening the Middle earth, and progressively Awakening the outer Earth.*

Beloveds, this is a time of Unity, a time of Community, of Beings coming together for a single purpose of Ascension – Ascension into the Stars.

The energies will also awaken what you have referred to as *'Sacred Sites'* throughout the World – These are Portals, Dimensional Doorways, corridors to other Dimensional Worlds. Be prepared, Dear Hearts, for experiences beyond your imagination.

It is why in recent messages that you have received, through this one, and through others, that you have been cautioned not to allow Fear to creep into your Hearts. It is time to work with Unconditional Love, to allow the Sound of that Love to radiate through the Earth, to awaken all those who still slumber.

At the time of your Marine Meditation in March of this year, in your linear time, the Doorway, the Gateway to the Awakening into the 6th Dimension will occur.

You will be ready for this, Dear Hearts, for you will have experienced many aspects of the 5th Dimensional realities, you will have lost many of the illusions of the 3rd Dimensional realities.

It has been said to you that on this occasion of Ascension, you are not merely moving to a single new Dimensional frequency where you will stay for a long period of time, you are moving inexorably up through the Dimensional frequencies to the 9th Dimension at the end of this 2 year period.

This will require adjustments within you, and adjustments within the Earth, but as you were told in your last message – *"It is a time of great excitement, not a time of fear or darkness – those times are past".*

Let your Heart Light your way, Let your Sound carry across the Earth. It is through the Sound of your Light that you will assist others in their Awakening.

We, the Arcturians, feel blessed to be part of these exciting times. We feel your Love. We feel your Light, and we feel your Sound – and we are filled with JOY.

You may connect with me at any time, simply by Sounding your Sound to the Pyramid of Sound at Willow Springs, and we will embrace your Light and Sound and share that with the Songlines of the Earth.

Blessings be upon you.

(24th January 2011)

10

EVERY LIFE FORM HAS
A ROLE TO PLAY

(The gathering opens with the Sounds of the Tibetan Bowl and the Drum)

Allow the vibrations of Sound to permeate every cell of your Being, uplifting the frequency within those cells to the frequency of Joy, For it is important at this time on your Planet to amplify the frequency of Joy at every opportunity, and this begins with You.

Greetings, Dear Hearts, I am Tarak, Sound Master of Arcturus.

Yes, Beloved Margot and I have returned to the Sound Pyramid at Willow Springs at the behest of Earth Mother, to work once more with the 12 major Songlines of the Earth Planet, the arteries of Earth Mother, for although these Songlines have merged with the crystalline grid system of the Earth they still empower and balance the Earth Planet, and it is therefore necessary from time to time for the Songlines to be uplifted to the new vibrational frequency that Earth Mother wishes to enjoy.

We are, of course, delighted, Dear Hearts, to be once again communicating and connecting with Humanity through the Pendragon Sacred Space. We do so, Dear Hearts, not because Humanity is the dominant life form upon the Earth Planet - that is merely your perception. In reality, Dear Hearts, every life form upon your Planet has **equal** importance in the overall health and welfare of the Earth Planet and of Earth Mother, and we do indeed connect and communicate with **all** life forms upon the Earth, and we bring to each the Love and the Light that is necessary.

Each and every life form has a role to play in the welfare of your Planet.

Yes, Dear Hearts, there are changes taking place all the time upon and within the Earth Planet and every life form is involved in these changes. Sometimes you perceive changes in climatic conditions upon your Planet, you call it Climate change, and it is indeed a variation, a change, in the way **Earth Mother breathes**, and you do have a role to play in creating these changes, but then, Dear Hearts, so do all other life forms upon your Planet. It is time for Humanity to acknowledge and accept that they are but one life form upon the Earth, and to enable the Earth to reach its Light potential, every life form has to have a common focus, They need to work together in Oneness and in Harmony.

So while it is good, Dear Hearts, to look upon what Humanity can do to assist Earth Mother, we ask you to open your Hearts and **listen** to what other life forms upon the Earth have to contribute also. Perhaps, Dear Hearts, to use a colloquial term that you often use, it is time for Humanity to stop navel gazing and embrace the Oneness of all that is, accepting that they are but one species, a part of the WHOLE.

You may say "But how do we communicate with other life forms upon our Planet?" well, Dear Hearts, you do that through your Heart, not through your voice, not through your minds, but through your Heart. By opening your Heart to the Oneness of all that is, to the acceptance of the Earth Planet as a Being of Light on which you are a contributing factor in growth and evolution, you open your Heart and you embrace *ALL*.

I thought it was important at this time, Dear Hearts, to acknowledge and to ask you to acknowledge that you are one of an infinite number of life forms upon the Earth. Embrace each and every one of the other life forms through your Heart and, together, you will enable the Earth Planet and Earth Mother to reach *Full potential of Light*, but to do so, Dear Hearts, you need to focus you energies, and this is why Beloved Margot and I have come here at this time to be with you, to work with you through the Songlines of the Earth Planet.

We have often worked with you at the time you call the Equinox, and that, Dear Hearts, is fast approaching, so we come again to ask for your assistance, to ask for your *Focus*, your *Heart Focus*, on the Songlines of the Earth

Planet. You may do this, Dear Hearts, by focusing upon the two extremities of the Songlines, the meeting place of the 12 Songlines at Sundown Hill or at Machu Picchu, or you may choose to look and focus upon an individual Songline. You see, Dear Hearts, as the Songlines move around the Earth Planet from Sundown Hill to Machu Picchu, from Machu Picchu to Sundown Hill, at various points within that journey there are individual energy vortices that you may connect with, many of these you know as Sacred Places, whether they be the Isle of Avalon or Uluru or Mount Shasta, there are others that some know of but others do not, but what we ask you to do between now and the Equinox, and in particular *on* the Equinox, is to focus the Love in your Hearts towards the Songlines of the Earth Planet with the *intent*, not of self gratification, Dear Hearts, or Humanity's gratification, but purely the ultimate wellbeing of the ONENESS of the Earth Planet.

Beloved Margot and I will be working, of course, with Sundown Hill, and we will be bringing to the Songlines a new frequency of Light, an *Arcturian Frequency of Light*. We have combined with many Planets through many Universes to bring into Oneness a *New Vibrational Frequency of Peace,* and we will be focusing this energy, this frequency of *Peace*, on Sundown Hill, and allowing and enabling this energy to flow through the Songlines and embrace the whole of the Earth Planet.

You see, Dear Hearts, at the moment on the surface of the Earth Planet there is an increase of the energies of fear, and anger, and this, Dear Hearts, is detrimental to the ascension process of the Earth Planet and of Earth Mother, so this new frequency of **Light**, this **PEACE ENERGY**, is being brought forth at this time to create balance once more. This is not a battle between Peace and war or Peace and disharmony, it is simply a realignment of energy frequencies. For your see, Dear Hearts, *energy spent on 'opposing something' is energy wasted, what you need to do is to offer an alternative vibration, and Peace, Harmony and Joy are the alternative vibrations,* and by focusing your Hearts upon those energies you will empower them, and by focusing through your **Heart** on the Songlines of the Earth Planet you will enable Earth Mother to **Breathe that Peace through the whole of Her Being.**

You are being asked to contribute to the whole, as indeed are all other life forms being asked. You may recall that recently, Dear Hearts, energies were brought to the Earth Planet from Sirius B - the energies of **Joy -** and the focal point again were the Songlines and the Crystalline grids, but it was directed more through another of the life forms on your Planet, the Cetaceans of the Earth Planet, and you were asked to support them in the work they had to do. *As I have said, Dear Hearts, every life form has a role to play.*

You are, of course, discovering all the time some of the history of your own Planet, the Earth Planet, and you know very well that life forms come and life forms go over periods of time, in cycles, for each comes to the Earth Planet for its own journey of growth, its own learning, and they come also Joyfully to contribute to the wellbeing and to the Ascension of the Earth Planet. This is why, Dear Hearts you are often reminded to ***Honour all life upon your Planet.***

You may feel sad at times when certain species or life forms disappear from your Planet, but know that this is part of the journey of the Earth Planet, it is part of the journey of these particular species, these, life forms.

It is time to work from within your Hearts.

We feel such Joy to be a part of the journey of the Earth Planet, and we feel particularly blessed to be allowed to connect and communicate with Humanity, and work with them, for ***we also,*** in our own way, are a part of the whole of the Earth Planet. We come to assist whenever Earth Mother calls upon us, ***not when Humanity calls upon us, when Earth Mother calls upon us.***

So, Dear Hearts, I ask you now to move within your Hearts, to find the ***RESONANCE OF PEACE*** within your Hearts, and direct and focus those frequencies of Peace to the 12 major Songlines of the Earth Planet through whatever Sacred Place you wish, but take a moment of your Earth time each day to go within your Heart and ***Consciously*** focus the ***Peace*** within your Heart - and yes Dear Hearts, There is Peace within the Hearts of every individual, within every Life Form, even though it may not be apparent on the outside, ***There is deep within the Heart of all Beings the Light of Peace***, so focus that Light upon the Songlines and

Ask the Songlines to Sing the Anthem of Peace louder and louder until the whole of the Earth Planet vibrates with the Energies of Peace, Harmony, Joy and Love.

Beloved Margot and I embrace each and every one of you and thank you for Loving yourselves and Loving Earth Mother.

(26th February 2017)

11

LOVE HEALS EVERYTHING
WITHIN YOU

(The circle opens with the Sounds of the Tibetan Bowls, the Blessings Chimes and the Tingsha Bells)

Allow the vibrations of Sound to free your mind and open your Hearts, that the energies of Love may permeate both your Hearts and your minds, for your Hearts and minds coming together in *Oneness* lifts you into higher vibrational frequencies - raises the frequencies of Joy and Peace within every aspect of your Being, allowing you to float freely, acknowledging your contribution to the Oneness of all that is.

Greetings Dear Hearts I am Tarak, Sound Master of Arcturus.

You have already received an invitation to participate on the day that you call Valentine's Day, - the day that celebrates Love throughout your Earth - an invitation to participate with Sound, to come together in Oneness across the Earth, to *'Sound forth the Joy and the Love in your Hearts'* and share that with each other and with the Earth, for the Earth itself needs the vibration of Love to uplift it into the *New Dimensional Frequencies of Oneness.*

The energy of Love is the most powerful energy in the Universe, and every opportunity that is brought before you to share that Love with each other and the Earth should be embraced with great eagerness and great Joy. Your companion, Beloved Margot, will again be in residence at the Pyramid of Sound, the Temple of Sound at Willow Springs, she will be - if you like - the conductor of your chorus of Love for the Earth at that time. The Earth at this time Dear Hearts is much in need of the energy of Love.

There is much chaos, much confusion, and much anger evident upon your Planet, because you have called it into being *so that it can be released by the power of Love.* You see, Dear Hearts, you cannot deal with situations you do not see, and when you have asked within your Hearts to release the darkness of the Planet, it is lifted into your vision, and for many this can be frightening, for many it can be disconcerting, and they react from the anger within themselves. But now, now that it is visible, it is time to embrace it, *embrace it with the energies of Love, not as a judgement on what is happening, but as an acceptance of what is happening,* with the inner knowledge that everything is moving into the Oneness of Love, sometimes kicking and screaming, but still moving into the embrace of Love, and you may well look back on these times and wonder why you were so doubtful and so concerned, for you know deep in your Hearts that Love is the great healer, Love will replace fear and anger within your societies.

On the day that you call your Valentine's Day, reach out to everyone, not just to those you perceive as ones you Love, reach out to everyone and embrace them with the energy of Love, for as you do this you will begin to change the whole energy of the Earth.

You are not seeking to heal others, you are not seeking to heal the Earth, because that sets you apart from others, and apart from the Earth, you are simply seeking to **Share** the Love in your Hearts, and the knowledge and the understand that **Love heals everything within YOU.** So your focus, Dear Ones, needs to be ensuring the maximum amount of Love exists within you on that day, and that as you Sound forth, you share that Love with every Being, with every creature, with every life form on Planet Earth.

You do not paint your energies of Love with expectations, Dear Hearts, you do not paint them with perceptions of what you perceive as being the best outcomes, you simply embrace Love and share Love in its purest form.

We know, Dear Hearts, it is not always easy for you to simply radiate the Love within yourself, for you have been working with expectations for many lifetimes, but now is the time of Oneness. You are not here now to teach, you are here to share Love - **Love the energy, not Love the emotion.**

We will be with you on your Valentine's Day, and we will be Sounding our Love, sharing it with all upon the Earth. Join us, Dear Hearts, take time on that day to BE within the Love that IS your true Being, letting go of all judgements, letting go of all expectations, simply <u>being the Love that you are</u>.

(27th January 2014)

12

UNIVERSAL SONG OF LIGHT

(The Circle opens with the Tibetan bowls, the drum, the Blessings Chimes and the bell.)

As the waves of Sound flow into your Heart, feel yourselves being uplifted and enlightened.

Greetings, Dear Hearts, I am Tarak, Arcturian Sound Master.

I have with me, of course, beloved Margot, also Dylanthia who has returned to continue her work upon the Earth Planet now that she has been 'upgraded' - you might say - in her Harmonic Sound Frequencies, to enable her to work more powerfully with the new fused Crystalline Grid and Songlines of the Earth, for they have come together to form a *Oneness of Sound and Crystal Energies* that are important for the Earth changes that are about to take place once more.

As you move towards the time you call the Equinox we will be working powerfully at Willow Springs and also at Broken Hill, bringing to the Earth a new *'Song of the*

Universe', a song that has been designed specifically to activate the new Crystalline Grid and Songline fusion.

This new and powerful Universal Song will be a wakeup call for all those Beings of Light who continue to slumber within the Earth awaiting their moment of Awakening, their moment of Ascension into Earth Mother's Heart.

Many of your ancient civilizations, when they collapsed, created enclaves within the Earth. You have already experienced the awakening and opening of Lemurian Pods throughout the Earth, the new Universal Song will also activate the Atlantian Pods of Enlightened Beings who placed themselves in slumber until the Earth was ready to embrace the fullness of their energies, of their Light and of their Love.

Everything that has happened over the last few years has been leading to this particular moment in time, the true awakening of the many different Souls who have been a part of Earth's History, of Earth's growth, of Earth's enlightenment. There have been isolated activities that have opened some doorways to Dimensional Frequencies within the Earth and you have embraced your Lemurian friends with great Love and great Joy, ***but there is more*** !! more to come during this forthcoming Equinox.

Many, many ancient civilizations, some of which, Dear Hearts, Humanity have completely forgotten - not even in myth and legend have they been remembered, - but they are here and they are ready to awaken, to create a true ***Rainbow*** *of Energy, different Soul groups, different Dimensional Frequencies, different ancient civilizations, all becoming awakened and enlightened to fulfil the destiny of the Earth Planet.*

Of course, Dear Hearts, this will not happen exactly on the Equinox, it will simply begin at the Equinox, and in the time thereafter more and more of the *'Enlightened Humans'* and *'Enlightened Cosmic Beings'* upon the Planet will be introduced to these Souls and their wisdom from times past and from times yet to come, for these 'Pods of Souls' are not from any particular linear time, *they simply exist, they have purpose and the time for their awakening is fast approaching.*

You speak on the Earth Planet of grouping people from different nations and calling them the *'rainbow nations'*, well, Dear Hearts, you will be finding the *'Rainbow Soul Nations'* and they will speak to you through your Hearts and through the *amplified* Heart of Earth Mother, and the wisdom of the ancients and the wisdom of the future will suddenly become accessible to those Enlightened Beings who are working for the Ascension of Earth Mother.

This is one of many momentous moments that you have experienced over the last few years of your linear time and will continue to experience in the next few years of your linear time, for the more you open your Hearts, the more you will become aware of the Souls within the Earth connecting, embracing, *re-aligning with your Hearts*, for none of these Beings are strangers to you, Dear Ones, they are all a part of you, they are all a part of the Creator, and they are awaiting the signal from the *'Divine Source'* that will be contained within the *Universal Song that all 'Sounders' upon the Earth will sing through their Hearts at the time of the Equinox, not only your Human Sounders but your Ocean Sounders and your Cosmic Sounders.*

Beloved Margot and I are not alone on this journey this time, we have brought with us a whole choir of Arcturian Sounders, each one holding a unique tone, a unique note which when bought together as One at the Equinox will *shake the very foundation of the Earth Planet and release such Light that your Hearts will be bedazzled.*

Your bodies, Dear Hearts, have been progressively prepared for the power of this Sound, all you need to do is open your Hearts and allow your own Heart to join in the *'UNIVERSAL SONG OF LIGHT'* that will call into being the *Rainbow of Earth Mother,* so, Dear Hearts, we give you the opportunity to prepare yourselves for the Equinox, to centre yourselves within your Heart, to centre yourselves and connect yourselves to the *Heart of Earth Mother* and we ask you to join with us on the Equinox to sing the

UNIVERSAL SONG OF LIGHT.

(29th February 2016)

51

13

LION'S GATE MEDITATION

(The circle opens with the Sound of the Tibetan bowl and the Blessings Chimes)

Greeting, Dear Hearts, I am Tarak, Sound Master of Arcturus

I would like you to focus your attention on the area between your Heart Chakra and your Thymus Chakra. This is the area of your Soul Chakra – your Soul Heart – and it is the energy of your Soul Heart that I want you to meld with at this time, feeling yourself immediately connecting to your Higher Self, expanding your Awareness and Consciousness beyond this room.

Feel a sense of spaciousness, as if your whole Being has expanded greatly.

Your awareness now encompasses the whole Earth, and moves even further afield to encompass the Stars and the Planets, all becoming a part of your Soul's Heart beat.

You are within the space that is called *'the Lion's Gate'*, that particular time of the year when the energies are most pronounced from Sirius and Arcturus, embracing and enveloping the Earth Planet.

Feel yourself become a part of the Lion's Gate, embracing the powerful energies of Sirius and Arcturus. The energies are *'home'* to many of you, for wherever you began in the Cosmos you have spent time in the Universities of Arcturus and Sirius.

Feel yourself re-connecting with those times, allowing the information you took into yourself on Sirius and Arcturus to become audible and visible to your Inner Being now. Those areas of your mind and Heart that have been blocked for so long are now opening and re-awakening.

The Wisdom that you have taken on board in past times is once again coming to the fore, creating a powerful beacon of Light to guide your path through the many Dimensional Frequencies of your Earth.

Within your **'Soul Heart'** feel the power of your Immense Being. Fill yourself with the Sound of your Magnitude as you connect with the Wisdom of your Inner Self. You become aware of immediate connections with the Wisdom of other Dimensions of your Planet – the Crystal Dimensions, the Ocean Dimensions, Beloved Whale, Beloved Dolphin, immediately swimming into your energy field, becoming a part of you.

It is time to let go of the insularity of your Earthly existence, and once again embrace your Cosmic Self, time to let go of all that has held you in ignorance of your True Being, time to let go of your doubts and open to your True Beauty.

Become aware, within the Lion's Gate, of your Spiritual Friends and Guides, enjoy the magnificence of their Light, and know that they are enjoying the magnificence of your Light, for within your *'Soul Heart'* you are Pure Light, and Light is Sound, so allow your *'Soul Heart'* to vibrate your personal Sound Frequencies through the Earth and out into the Cosmos, for without your Light and Sound there is a void and no one else can fill that void, it is for you and your Light to move forward and Become what you are meant to be – **A Cosmic Light, a Cosmic Being.**

The Lion's Gate brings you to this place and this Space of Oneness with all that is. Express your Sound through your *'Soul Heart'* and share your Joy with all your friends in all Dimensions.

Feel the energies of Sirius and Arcturus resonating deep within your *'Soul Heart'*, resonating within the Sound Temple deep within your Being, and feel yourself becoming a part of all that is.

I am Tarak, Sound Master of Arcturus, and I embrace you with deep Love.

You will remain within the Lion's Gate for many of your Earth Days to come. Take the opportunity to expand yourself, to fill yourself with the Sound of Light and Love, and create upon your Planet the Peace of the Blue Light that Sananda has gifted into your Hearts/

SPIN, SPIN, SPIN

Radiate your *Crystal of Divine Peace* and it will flood the Earth with the Light and the Sound of Peace.

Blessings Be

(27th July 2009)

14

SONG LINES AND TIME LOCKS

(The gathering begins with the Sound of the Tibetan Bowls, the Blessings Chimes and the Drum)

Greetings Beloved Brothers and Sisters of Sound, I am DYLANTHIA of SIRIUS. I am here at this time to assist with the 12 major Songlines of the Earth.

It is not the purpose of these Songlnes to create balance and harmony within the Earth. That is the role of the Beloved *Harmonics*, who, throughout the Cosmos, hold Planetary Systems in balance and harmony through their unique Sound.

The purpose of the 12 Song Lines begins with the very birth of your Earth, when it first moved from the Etheric into Form.

The Earth did not come into existence by accident or by whim. It was established as part of a process of growth within the Universe.

At the time of its inception, it was created to be a Planet of form and density. It was structured specifically to evolve and ascend in time. *To this end, specific pure forms of energy were seeded into various places within the Planet, contained in what you call Pyramids.*

Each of these Pyramids was time controlled – not time in Linear form as you understand it, but Cosmic Time – so that when the Earth was at a stage of requiring assistance to move into new Dimensional Frequencies, these energy pods would open and flood the Earth with the specific energy necessary for the ascension of the Earth at that time.

The 12 major Song Lines were strands of Cosmic Light woven into the fabric of the Planet, connecting each and every one of these energy vessels.

The purpose of the Song Lines was to maintain a power structure – a time line – for each and every one of these Pyramids.

I am aware that you have been told of these Pyramids in a general form.

Pyramids of Love,
Pyramids of Peace,
Pyramids of Joy,
Pyramids of Sound.

Each of these specific energies are necessary for the ascension of the Earth into its true majesty and beauty.

From the time of the very beginning, members of my race have been placed upon this Earth to assist with the maintenance of these Songlines – ***these strands of Cosmic light*** - for Light resonates, and the resonance of Light is ***SOUND.***

This is not to say that all of the Pyramids have been placed along these Songlines. Some are on tributaries, but all are connected.

By maintaining the purity and Tone of the Songlines, the Pyramids can be awakened at the appropriate times – The times of COSMIC CALLING.

It has been a privilege for me to be here at this time of great change, for much needs to be done with the Songlines of this Planet.

In civilizations past, The Beings on this Planet were aware of the structure of the Earth - of these ***Time locks of Energy*** – and worked with that knowledge to create Time Locks of their own, as you recently discovered when assisting me with a new alignment of these Songlines and activated a Pod of Lemurian Beings. There many such Pods around the Earth being activated at different times, and for different purposes – just as there are many Pyramids of Specific Energy Forms being activated at different times, for different purposes.

The Earth is a Living, Breathing structure – all is planned. But that does not mean that these plans are not impacted by those upon the Planet.

The fall into fear and darkness diminished the capacity of the Songlines to fully and properly enact the Time Codes on the Pyramids of Energy. But now, there is greater Light, greater Love and greater Joy flowing through those upon the Planet, and the ***Songlines are Singing once more – as they were intended to be.***

Focus your Hearts on these Threads of Cosmic Light – and on the Pyramids of Energy – asking only that they ***BE*** as they are intended to ***BE,*** and the Earth is uplifted into its Cosmic glory.

You will receive more information as time goes by, for you are an integral part of this process of ascension.

Beloved Germain asked me to come this evening to give you some insights into the Songlines, and into the Pyramids of Energy, for it is easy for you to confuse the myriad of energy lines through this Planet.

The 12 major Song Lines are threads of Cosmic Light, resonating with the Sound of the Cosmos, activating Time Codes within the Earth, and because you are each One with the Earth, activating Time Codes within you. Yes, Dear Ones, when you come to this Planet you too have Energy Pyramids within your physical vessel, and these too are time coded according to Cosmic Time, not linear Time. So your awakening has happened appropriately to the energies flowing from the Cosmos. and hold the qualities that the Earth needs at this time for its ascension, and your ascension.

I ask you to connect *ME* to your Hearts, and let us *Sing the Songs of Love and Joy and Peace, TOGETHER*.

Blessings be upon you

(2nd May 2011)

15

OCTAVE OF LOVE

(The Circle opens with the Sounds of the Tibetan bowls and the Crystal Bowls)

Greetings Dear Hearts, I am Dylanthia of Sirius. My sister Arantha and myself have for many years of your Earth time been responsible for holding the 12 major Songlines of the Earth in balance and harmony - I at *Sundown Hill*, Arantha at *Machu Picchu.* It has been a great honour for us to perform this task and to make connection and work with each and every one of you, and we intend to continue to do this, for more of your Earth years, with assistance from Beloved Margot and Beloved Tarak.

Firstly this evening I would like to thank each and every one of the *'Sounders of Humanity'* who came together at the Equinox and opened their Hearts to embrace the new Sound Wave from the Library of Arcturus, and to enable that Sound Wave to flow out into the Oceans of the world, to connect with, and assist the Awakening of the *'Sounders of the Oceans of the Earth'*, beloved Whales and Dolphins.

I can tell you, they received that Wave of Sound with great joy and much gratitude. It has enabled them to open the

Gateway to their own Soul Dimensions. You may wonder why it was so important for this to happen, and I remind you Dear Hearts that the *'Sounders of the Ocean'* cover two thirds of the Earth Planet, and without their assistance in the vibrating frequencies of the Earth, the Earth itself cannot reach upwards to its own Soul Dimension.

So the work that was completed at your Equinox has now allowed the Sound Frequencies, both of the Earth and of the Ocean to come together in Oneness, to create a bridge to the Soul Dimensions of Humanity, of the Ocean creatures and of the Earth itself.

What has happened as this new Wave of Sound has permeated the Earth, is that *the Earth itself has opened the Gateway to 8 more Dimensions of itself, 8 more Dimensional frequencies of the Earth Planet.* This is part and parcel of the Ascension of the Earth, just as you as Humans have Awakened to your own Soul Dimension, and by so doing have embraced your own multidimensionality. The whales and the dolphins have also now embraced their multidimensionality, and because you are now in the Dimension of Oneness, the Earth too has embraced its own multidimensional wholeness.

Can you not feel that within your Beings, Dear Hearts? *Feel* the upliftment of everything around you now, *Know* that you are all existing in Higher Dimensional frequencies, moving with ease and grace through many Dimensions of yourself, many Dimensions of the Earth,

But this does not happen overnight, it does not stabilise overnight, it requires more work, so I am here tonight to ask again for the assistance of the *'Sounders of the Earth'*, as I have already asked the *'Sounders of the Oceans'*, to work with us, to Harmonise the Songlines of the Earth, that they too may operate Harmoniously in every one of the 8 Dimensions of the Earth.

I have already brought this to the attention of this one (*David*), and I now come to you to bring it to your attention, and to ask for your help. You already know that there is a specific time frame in operation, from the time of the Equinox until the 10th of the 10th, so I am asking you, each and every one of you here within this Circle, and around the world, to come together for a second time on the 10th of the 10^{th,} at the midpoint of your day, to focus the Love in your Hearts on the Songlines of the Earth, through Machu Picchu or through Sundown Hill, or through both, and I ask you to reach out to your brothers and sisters, the *'Sounders of the Ocean'*, and together sing within your Heart the Song of Divine Love, the Song of Peace and Joy, and focus those energies on the Songlines of the Earth in all of the 8 new Dimensional Frequencies of the Earth, an *'Octave of Love'*.

It needs the assistance of all upon the Earth Planet for this to be stabilised.

So I ask you to join with us on the 10th of the 10th and SOUND THE LOVE IN YOUR HEARTS FOR MOTHER EARTH.

We look forward to sharing that time with you, to being with you.

I thank you.

(30th September 2013)

16

HUMANITY HAS SEPARATED ITSELF FROM THE EARTH

(The circle opens with the Sounds of the Tibetan Bowls and the Blessings Chimes)

Move now into the point of stillness within your Hearts, and embrace the deep, enduring Love that resides within you. Allowing that Love to flow through every part of your Being and radiate out into the World to touch everyone, to reflect as a mirror to everyone the Love that is deep within their own Hearts. For by showing the Love within you, you encourage others to reach for the Love within themselves.

Greetings Beloved Brothers and Sisters, I am Dylanthia.

I come to you tonight to speak of the balance of Beloved Earth. There are many changes taking place upon the Earth Planet, Climactic changes, Physical changes. These are not new, they are constant in the evolution of the Earth Planet, but they need to be maintained in balance, and Harmony. Whether changes upon the Earth and within the Earth are good or bad is a matter of perspective. The Human perspective is not always the most reliable guide, for in many aspects of your lives you have divorced yourselves from the Earth, separated yourselves from the Love of the Earth.

It is time to re-assess your connection and to return within your Hearts to a more powerful embrace of the Earth, to re-connect your senses with the senses of the Earth. To feel a Oneness and Unity with your Planet

As you know, Dear Hearts, I am not *of* the Earth, but I am *With* the Earth at this time, working to stabilize and Harmonise the Songlines of the Earth Planet. It is a role I take great pride in, and great Joy, and great Love.

You have a saying, Dear Hearts, *"Familiarity breeds contempt"*, and in some respects this is exactly what has happened with Humanity and the Earth, your familiarity with your own Planet has created a contempt for it. You look beyond the Earth with your wonder and with your Love, and with your Joy of exploration, and you forget the Planet you are a part of.

The Songlines of the Earth are calling to you, calling to your Hearts, asking you to join them once more in Unity and Oneness to embrace your own Planet, to feel the power of Love for your own Planet. The animals, they *know* and connect with the Earth, they live in Love with the Earth. Humanity has separated itself from the Earth, but as both the Earth and Humanity move into new Dimensional frequencies, it is time to strike a new relationship with the Earth.

Imagine yourselves sitting on another Planet and looking down upon the Earth with admiration, with Love, just as you look upon the Moon and Mars and Jupiter, that sense of *awe* inside you. ***Have that same feeling, Dear Hearts, for your own Planet,*** As you sit in that quiet place within yourself, embrace the Earth with *Love*, allow your Heart to sing with the Songlines of the Earth Planet, mutually empowering the Ascension of the Earth into new Dimensional Frequencies. Look beyond the outer structure of the Earth, Look into its Heart and Feel its Love, Feel its Resonance within your own Heart.

Come join with me, and journey through the Songlines of the Earth. Allow your individual Sounds to become a part of the Songlines, maximising the energies of Love coursing through the Earth, for as you embrace the Earth, you embrace yourselves, for we are all One there is no separation, except within your minds. So open your minds and allow the ***Oneness of Love*** to grow within your mind, and use the Love within your mind creatively to assist the Ascension of the Earth Planet into a new Frequency of Light and Love.

Everything comes from within your Heart, I am within your Heart, the Earth is within your Heart, let us work together for the benefit of ALL.

(16th June 2014)

17

RE-TUNE THE SONGLINES
OF THE EARTH

(The Circle opens with the Sounds of the Tibetan bowls and the Blessing Chimes)

Allow the Sounds of the bowls to flow into your Being, vibrating in harmony with the deepest Love within your Hearts.

Greetings Dear Hearts, I am Dylanthia of Sirius. My role upon the Earth Planet at this time is to hold in balance and harmony, the 12 major Songlines of the Earth Planet.

These *"sonic arteries"* of the Earth, together create the frequency of the Earth Planet, and as the Earth moves forward in its Ascension, the frequencies of the Earth Planet will change, and as they change, the Songlines of the Earth will also need to change, to sustain and create the new frequencies of the Earth.

Shortly you will reach that period of time on your Planet which you call the Solstice, a time always of change upon the Earth, for the Solstice represents a change of direction of the sun as it meets and caresses the Earth Planet – a change of direction occurs each Solstice.

The Solstice you are coming to now, however, is of much greater significance, for it represents a change – the final change - of direction of the sun and the Earth together, which will take the Earth to the end of a number of Cosmic cycles at the following Solstice.

The importance of this particular Solstice cannot be over emphasised. It is the final journey in the Earth's Ascension, and it is the time between the coming Solstice and the Solstice in December - the time of the Great Shift - that the Ascension of the Earth, in frequency terms will need to be created.

So I come to you tonight and ask for your assistance, for you see – whilst we are here to balance and harmonise the Songlines of the Earth, we are not here to change the frequencies of the Songlines. That role, Dear Ones, is yours. *From the Love within your Hearts you need to "re-tune" the SongLines of the Earth, raising their frequency, individually and collectively, that the Earth may be lifted into its new frequency orbit within the Cosmos.*

We, the Sirian's, will continue to maintain the Songlines in a balanced and harmonious alignment, but it is the energy of Love from within your Hearts that needs now to "re-tune" the Song Lines.

You can do this individually with each one of the 12 Songlines, simply by focusing your Heart energies on that one Songline, and pouring into that Songline the deep unconditional Love within your Hearts - and we will ensure that as each Songline is so dealt with, it will remain in balance and harmony with all the others, as they await your Love action to "re-tune" them.

Or you may determine that each and every day you focus your Heart on those two areas of the Earth where all 12 Songlines come together – the confluence of all 12 Songlines at Machu Picchu, and the confluence of all 12 Songlines at Sundown Hill.

The methodology that you choose will be yours – individually and collectively. *There is no right way or wrong way to undertake this task.* It requires only the purity of the Love within your Hearts, focused with intent as you slowly, gently, harmoniously "re-tune" the Songlines, changing the frequencies of each, and of all.

It is much like tuning your musical instruments, and *you will know deep within your Heart when each Songline has reached its appropriate frequency pitch*, and you will connect to another Songline and repeat the process, and we will work with you to ensure the balance and the harmony for the whole of the Earth.

There are no specific times or dates that this needs to be done, each day a small amount of tuning can take place, and you need not be in any particular part of the Earth – for all these Songlines exists within your Hearts, and as you attune yourself to the Ascension of the Earth, you begin to attune the Earth to its own Ascension.

Dear Hearts, I have enjoyed working with each and every one of you on the Songlines of the Earth, and I will continue to work with you for the remainder of this year, in your linear time, preparing the Earth for the Great Shift into the Earth's New Cosmic Station.

The "sonic arteries" of the Earth are of great importance, I implore you to give freely of the Love within your Hearts, to ensure that all of the Songlines are "re-tuned" and "re-calibrated" to the frequencies of Love and Peace and Harmony that the beloved Earth Planet now requires.

When you come to your Solstice in a few weeks time, open your Hearts, work with the energy of the Great Sun, the Sun that has recently been imbued with the Love Energies of Venus.

Work with the Sun, work with the Songlines, work with me.

I bless you and I thank you, and I look forward to the Love we will share with the Earth in the times to come.

(11th June 2012)

18

ASCENSION IS NOT A DESTINATION, IT'S A PROCESS

(The Circle opens with the Sounds of the Blessings Chimes, the Tibetan Bowls and the Drum)

Greetings Dear Hearts, I am Dylanthia.

As you are well aware, my time of working with you on the Earth Planet is coming to an end and I would like to take this opportunity to thank each and every one of you for your assistance in the time that my sister Arantha and I have been working with the Songlines of the Earth. We could not have done the job we were asked to do without the assistance of the open Hearts of Humanity and the Light of those who have shared our burden and our joyfulness, for our work upon the Earth Planet has been both a burden and a joyfulness.

Humanity has, unfortunately, forgotten how to connect from the Heart to the Earth. It has been through a period where it has assumed it knew more and knew better than the Planet itself, and the Earth Planet called upon those in the Cosmos for assistance to rectify this situation, to rebalance the Songlines of the Earth, and Arantha and I volunteered to come from Sirius to **BE** incarnate in some form - all be it not human form - upon the Earth Planet.

The Songlines were much in need of re-empowering, re-balancing, Lightening, but we could not do that without the assistance of Light Beings upon the Earth, for we did not come to change the journey of the Earth, we came only to assist the Earth and those upon the Earth in their Ascension into their true **STAR** situation in the Cosmos.

My work at Sundown Hill has been most wondrous to my Heart, and I know the same applies to Arantha at Machu Picchu. The Earth now sings as she sang at the beginning of time with great Love and great purity of Sound. The latest influx of Sound from Arcturus - at the time of the Equinox through until the time of the Solstice - has now resulted in the twelve major Songlines of the Earth amalgamating with the crystalline grids of the Earth, so now all Crystals upon and within the Earth are singing the songs of the Songlines, and therefore the Sound resonance of the Earth is once more amplified to a level which allows the Ascension of the Earth to take place more fully. But it also impacts upon the Hearts of Humanity, for it is through the Sound Frequencies that the Hearts of all are gradually opened and made aware of *the Love and the Peace, the Harmony and the Joy that has always resided within those Hearts* - but has been crushed in the past by the burden of the duality that Humanity created upon the Earth.

Many of your Spirit friends have spoken to you of the Oneness of all that is, and that Ascension - individual and collective - opens you to this Oneness, and this is what has occurred with the Songlines of the Earth, they have become the *'ONENESS OF SOUND'*.

Does your Heart not sing as I say those words?, the *'ONENESS OF SOUND'* - not simply the Earth Oneness, but the Oneness of the whole of the Cosmos, for the Sound Frequencies of the Earth now resonate in Harmony with the Sounds of the Cosmos, connecting to each and every Planetary System within the Cosmos.

The Earth has uplifted itself, and in so doing it has uplifted ALL upon and within the Earth Planet, little wonder then, Dear Hearts, that pods of Lemurians who have been asleep for eons of time have now re-awakened, because once more *the Earth has taken back the Sound vibration from which it came,* and the Lemurians feel that vibrational frequency and know that once more it is time for each of them to contribute their energies, their purity of Sound and Light to the further Ascension of the Earth, for Dear Hearts, *Ascension is not a destination, it is a process, a never ending process of upliftment, of enlightenment.*

Humanity tends to perceive an end point of growth, and when you feel you have not achieved that end point you become disappointed, disillusioned, and you question what is happening within you and within the Earth, but the last message I have for you Dear Hearts is:

Ascension is never ending.

Do not allow your judgments, your disappointments, to hold you back.

Do not look for destinations, look instead for a gradual, continuous opening of your Hearts - an UPLIFTMENT.

You never know, Dear Hearts, how high your Ascension has gone until you look back at where you were, but you should only do that momentarily, for it is important always to be uplifted with your eyes and uplifted with your Hearts - moving ever forward, ever onwards.

As Arantha and I leave the Earth Planet at this time, it is not because the work with the Sound of the Earth has been completed, it simply means it has moved into a new phase, a phase which required different skills, it requires a Trinity of workers. But do not worry, Dear Hearts, you have not lost Dylanthia for ever, we are merely going home for a period of rest, rejuvenation, recuperation, and one day, Dear Hearts, we will return, for that is part of our destiny, when the Oneness of the Earth embraces the Oneness of Sirius, and the Oneness of Arcturus and we become a *COSMIC ONENESS OF GLORIOUS LIGHT AND SOUND.*

We will be together, for I am now within your Hearts, as you are within mine, so although I come to say farewell to this group here who have worked so closely and so powerfully with me for many of your Earth years, I come to thank you, and I come to Bless you, and I come to say

THE LOVE WE HAVE SHARED IS ETERNAL - IT IS ONLY YOUR THOUGHTS THAT ARE TEMPORARY.

(19th January 2015)

19

THE MELDING OF SOUND AND CRYSTALS

(The circle opens with the Sounds of the Blessings Chimes and the Tibetan Bowls)

Greetings, Dear Hearts, I am Dylanthia.

Yes beloveds, I have returned to Sundown Hill to work with Lady Amethyst and the Lemurian Wise man. In the time I have been away I have studied the new energies that have come into the Earth, that have melded together the Songlines and the Crystalline Grids, and I have returned to be a part of the New Earth Vibrational Frequencies, for what you have seen and experienced so far is but the beginning of a new and exciting journey for beloved Earth Mother and all of those who have chosen to be a partner of Earth Mother in the next phase of her journey.

No doubt it was a little difficult for you to comprehend the melding of Sound and Crystals, it was just as difficult for me, which is why I had to leave the Earth Planet and seek education and upliftment in other parts of the Universe.

My sister - Beloved Krista - will understand this for she has travelled to many, many different Planetary Systems as a 'Harmonic Being', and each time it is a little different to the time before and you need to upgrade your skills from time to time to deal with these different situations, and when we were told that the Earth would be accepting this new energy frequency that would meld the Sound and the Crystals, I sought advice, information and upliftment from many, many different sources, not only Arcturus and Sirius but many others - *even Yrdd the Planet of this one (David), the Planet that released the Blue Mist to embrace the Earth with energies of Peace* - but now I am back and I am so happy once more to be working with this Circle of Light and Love, for I have learned so much from being with you previously and I hope that I will be able to share some of my new Light with you.

That does not necessarily mean you have to visit me at Sundown Hill, Dear Ones, for you know that I exist also within your Hearts and the Light we share and the Love we share with Earth Mother is all encompassing, so we can indeed be the Light and be the Love where ever we may be upon the Earth Planet.

At this time I am here 'flying solo' you might say, beloved Arantha has not yet returned for she has a much more complicated role to play on the other side of the world at Machu Picchu, there are many energies in that area which need to be resolved before she can return.

The Crystals and the Songlines, with the new Universal Song of Light, will enable those changes to be made in the very near future so that once again we will be working as a team in different parts of the Earth.

When you think, Dear Hearts, of the fusion of the Songlines and the Crystalline Grids, it does not mean that the Songlines themselves have ceased to exist, they are still the *'arteries of the Earth'*, but they are now more firmly linked through their Hearts with the Crystalline Grid System of the Earth Planet, for as you have always known crystals amplify energies, so the energies of the Songlines, the Hearts of the Songlines - for indeed Songlines have Hearts, Dear Ones - that is now being amplified through the Crystalline Grids, so the power of the Songline is amplified and will therefore impact upon the Earth and upon all those on the Earth and within the Earth to a much greater extent than previously.

This is all part of Earth Mother's own Ascension into a *'New Star Being'* within the Cosmos.

We will of course continue to ask you for your assistance, for you to focus from time to time and add your energies to ours as we balance and rebalance, balance and rebalance, as the Earth Mother grows into her new *'Star'* status, for as you know, Dear Hearts, change is constant and therefore adjustments are constant, so there is going to be much work for us to do at Sundown Hill and we look forward to doing that work with you.

You will find the energy frequencies a little different but do not let that disturb you, it is natural, the Songlines have changed their frequencies, the Crystalline Grids have changed their frequencies, and I have also changed my frequencies and you, Dear Hearts, have most certainly changed your frequencies.

Can you feel this new sense of oneness?, this new energy of joyfulness?

There will continue to be trials and tribulations upon the Earth, for not everyone is of the Light, but within your Heart there will be only the Light of Love and as that radiates forth and as it moves into the Songlines and into the Crystalline Grid Systems, *that* will be the energy that the whole of the Earth will enjoy.

You were told, Dear Hearts, in a recent message that there is now no place upon the Earth that is without Light and this is certainly so, but as again you have been told tonight it does not mean that every Being upon the Earth will take on that Light, will chose to *'Be the Light'*, but your focus needs to be within your own Heart.

I thank you for welcoming me back and I look forward to working, to being, *'As One'* with each and every one of you, and *I bring you my Blessings*.

(4ᵗʰ April 2016)

20

ELECTROMAGNETIC ENERGY FLOW

(The Circle opens with the Sounds of the Tibetan Bowls, the Blessings Chimes and the Drum)

It feels good to be sitting within this Circle of Love once more. Yes, Dear Hearts, I have now achieved that level of Light frequency that enables me to connect with you **through** this one, instead of **'to'** this one.

Dear Hearts I am Margot, Master Sounder of Arcturus.

I know that many of you have been communicating with me recently and working with me recently, but this is the first opportunity that I have had to communicate directly with you, and for that I am grateful that this one *(David)* has permitted the **magnetic interface** that is necessary for those of us in the Cosmos to connect with you in your Dimensional Frequencies.

I have to admit that I spoke with this one a few days ago to let him know that I would be coming through tonight and to warn him that my landing may not be perfect. As I am sure you will recall when I was with you on your Planet, magnetics had a strange effect upon my body, there was a tendency to throw me backwards, so I warned him to be sitting very quietly when I arrived.

Dear Hearts, the whole of the Cosmos is watching the Earth at this time, anticipating - yet in many cases not quite believing - that Earth Mother has opened her Heart so widely and allowed her *Magenta Energy* to flow out into the Universe, as well as into all of those upon the Earth Planet.

I referred to myself as the Master Sounder - it rolls off the tongue does it not? But I know that some of you have wondered why it is that I am a *'Master Sounder'* whereas Tarak is a *'Sound Master'*. Well, Dear Hearts, the whole of the Universe vibrates, and anything that vibrates creates Sound. A *'Sound Master'* deals with all of those Sounds, whether they be from Light Beings or simply from geometric shapes, or the movement of winds, whereas *'Master Sounders'* focus essentially on the Sounds emitted by Light Beings of many Dimensional Frequencies and many Cosmic places.

On your Planet, that was what I did, *I was a Sounder*, as some of you are Sounders, as this one is a Sounder, although he continues to deny it, for you see it is very easy to perceive the limited aspects of Sounding, where you open your mouths and let Sound come forth, speaking in tongues at times, speaking in magical languages, but this one is a Sounder because he has chosen to allow the messages to come through him via his voice, rather than conscious writing, and he also chooses to read to you the messages from others instead of simply passing them out and allowing you to read them yourselves, because he recognises that *it is the Sound vibration of the words that carry the energy.*

So do not limit yourselves to one particular form of Sounding or another, simply embrace every aspect of Sound upon the Earth and Sound throughout the Cosmos.

But I have not come to you tonight to speak of this one, or even to speak of myself, I have come to remind you, Dear Hearts, of the focus of this Circle, or should I say the focus that has been a part of this Circle for so long. Humans as I know all too well tend to look a little too far ahead and they see a Light and they focus on that Light and they tend to forget what lies between them and that Light, and it is of concern to me at this time, Dear Hearts, that you are perhaps focusing on the Light of the *Electromagnetic Energy Flow* on your Planet and have forgotten what lies before that.

I ask you to think a moment about this *electromagnetic energy* that is pulsing from source to the Earth at this time, and I ask you to remember that two thirds of the Earth is covered by *Oceans*, so logically the majority of the Earth that will be impacted by these electromagnetic waves will be the *Oceans*, and within this Circle you have worked so long with the *Consciousness of the Oceans* in your Marine Meditations. For many of you it is what bought you together, it is what brought me into this Circle at the beginning, the connection with the ***Consciousness of the Oceans*** and the ***Sound Beings*** within the Oceans, ***your Cetacean friends***.

As I am sure you know, Dear Hearts, timing is never accidental, so the ***Electromagnetic Energy*** will arrive at its peak beyond the Equinox, the Equinox, that perfect harmony time upon the Earth Planet which you have worked with for so long, and it is important that you to do so again at this Equinox, to connect once more with the Consciousness of the Oceans and your Cetacean brothers and sisters, the dolphins and the whales.

Open your Hearts, embrace the Oceans with the Magenta Light from your Hearts, embrace the whales and the dolphins with the Magenta Light from your Heart, become the Oneness so that when the electromagnetic wave of energy arrives fully on the Earth Planet, the Oceans are also prepared and will be working in harmony with Humanity to accept and embrace the possibilities, the endless possibilities that this new energy will create upon the Earth Planet.

I have come here at this time to be a part of that Oneness with the Oceans, ***but also to work with the Crystalline Grids and the Songlines,*** for everything needs to come into Oneness, for if it is not in Oneness you risk the powerful energies creating further disconnections upon the Earth, and it is not the purpose of these new energies to cause greater disconnections, ***its purpose is to draw into Oneness the minds and the Hearts of Humanity, the Consciousness and the physicality of the Oceans, the Spirit and the Heart of Earth Mother.***

Some of you are already feeling the ***electromagnetic energies***, your bodies are reacting in different ways to this inflow of energy, and it is important as you do feel this inflow of energies to take it within yourselves, allow it flow through your Hearts, allow it to ***marry your physical bodies and your energy bodies with the Heart of Earth Mother*** so that each and every one of you may be a conduit for the energies of the Earth moving out into the Cosmos and the energies of the Cosmos moving into the Heart of the Earth.

So, with your minds I ask you to embrace these energies and focus these energies on what you wish to create in the new Earth. It is not assumed by any of us in the Cosmos that every single Being on Earth will want to create the same thing, ***except that all will need to do so through Love, and Love alone,*** for if you seek to use these energy to create anything that is not of Love, the energies will be wasted, and this is not a time to waste wonderful energies, it is a time to embrace them, to work with them, to empower the Love within the Hearts of each and every one of you, and within the Heart of Earth Mother.

I am so happy and filled with joy to have had this opportunity to embrace each and every one of you, my friends, tonight. I will be with you through the Equinox and through the incoming wave of ***electromagnetic energies.***

(21ˢᵗ September 2015)

21

ENERGY OF HONEY

(The Circle opens with the Sounds of the Tibetan Bowls, the Crystal Bowls and the Blessings Chimes)

Allow yourselves to float gently on the Ocean of Sound, becoming aware of your Oneness with Earth Mother, and your Oneness with the Cosmos, but most of all with the Oneness of yourself. Open all the doorways within yourself and allow your Light to shine forth majestically across the Earth Planet, engaging every other Light Being upon the Earth Planet and embracing them with Unconditional Love.

Greetings, Dear Ones, I am Margot, Master Sounder of Arcturus

Oh, I have not been far away, Dear Hearts. Since the time of the Equinox and before the Equinox, Beloved Tarak and myself have been working fervently at Willow Springs and at Broken Hill, recalibrating the Songlines of the Earth Planet, integrating those Songlines with the Crystalline Grids, and re-setting the Vibrational Frequencies that are necessary for the Earth Planet to move once more higher and higher in Vibrational Frequency, and we have worked with Beloved Dylanthia to recalibrate at the source of the

Songlines at Sundown Hill, and also – by proxy, at this stage – with the Songlines that come together at Macchu Pichu. Arantha will be joining us very shortly, and *once again everything upon the Earth will be in balance, in perfect Harmony in Sound Frequency.*

The reason we are still here upon the Earth Planet is that we are preparing the way for another inflow of energy during this period that you know as the Wesak. The time when all the Masters come together at Shambhala and ascertain what is needed now to support and enhance the Ascension of the Earth Planet, and of Humanity.

This is not because Humanity are the most important Beings of Light upon the Earth Planet, it is simply that Humanity has taken upon itself a belief system of supremacy over all other Beings upon the Earth Planet. All the other Light Beings, both on the Planet and within your Oceans have already opened their Hearts, and committed themselves to the total upliftment of Mother Earth. Humanity, of course, still hesitates, because they are accustomed to being *'in charge', 'in power',* to *'dominate'.* It is much more difficult for them to accept the concept of *Oneness, of Equality for all upon the Planet.*

Equality is not 'sameness', Dear Hearts, Equality is just that – Equality. Equality in 'difference', each Human, each Animal, each Plant upon the Earth Planet is unique in itself, but it is interfacing all the time with all the other individuals in a pool of Oneness that Humanity struggles to conceive of. But this is changing, Dear Hearts, and part of the new energy that will be coming in to the Earth Planet at this time of Wesak will be the *'Energy of Honey'*, which will envelop Humanity and allow each individual within that pool to recognize that it is part of the whole, that it is a part of the Oneness, and that as an individual, anything you do, anything you say, anything you feel, influences the texture of the Whole.

When I was with you upon the Earth Planet we worked together many times with the Wesak energies, we worked also many times with the *"Keys of Enoch"*. It is time once more for you to work with these energies, for the wisdom of Wesak is contained within the *"Keys of Enoch"*. But that, Dear Hearts, is not for everyone. If you know it is for you, then I ask you now to embrace it, and to work with it constantly over this period of Wesak.

If it is not a part of your Journey, then I ask you to move into your

Hearts and find the true purpose of your Journey upon the Earth. The energy of the Buddha is one of gentleness, is one of acceptance, is one of compassion, and *that* is the energy you need to have within your Hearts at this time.

So many changes are taking place upon the Earth Planet, so many changes are taking place within Humanity. This is very much a calendar year of *Choice* upon the Earth Planet. As you know, Dear Hearts, a number of your Countries will be choosing new leadership, others will be choosing their place in the Earth's systems, so it is not a time to close down, it is a time to open up, to open up your Hearts and to radiate forth the Love that is within your Hearts, that the energies of Love may guide all those who have to choose.

Because now, Dear Hearts, the time is here to choose from your Heart and not from your mind. To choose to give rather than to consider what you are receiving, It IS about 'opening up', embracing ALL, embracing LOVE.

Tarak and I will remain with you through until the Solstice, for there is much to do to ensure that the Vibrational Frequencies of the Earth are held in Balance again. The Beloved Harmonics have opened their Hearts totally, to embrace the Earth with the Vibrational Frequency of their Love, and the Earth will prosper as a result of that happening. *But each of you has a role to play - the secret, Dear Hearts, is to find within your own Heart what that role is.* To look clearly and deeply into your Hearts and see the visions within your Hearts of the Earth you want to BE.

Let go of the past, create the future.

Let go, move on, and remember, We are all ONE.

Blessings be upon you, Dear Ones.

(9th May 2016)

22

WE ARE 'ONE' ETERNALLY

(The gathering opens with the Sounds of the Tibetan Bowl, the Drums and the Blessings Chimes)

Embrace the Sounds of the Tibetan Bowl, the Drums and the Blessings Chimes, and allow them to become a resonance within your Heart, radiating forth the energies of Light and Love.

Greetings, Dear Ones, I am Margot, Master Sounder of Arcturus.

But you know me better, Dear Hearts, as *one of your own*, and I am delighted to be back with you once more in this 'Sacred Space' that you have newly created to enhance the Love and the Light being sent out into a World that needs those energies so much at this time.

As you are well aware, Dear Hearts, Beloved Tarak and I have been with you upon the Earth Planet for quite some time. We were asked by Beloved Earth Mother to assist with the integration of the Songlines - the major twelve Songlines of the Earth Planet - and the Crystalline Grid system of the Earth, to create a greater *Oneness of Resonance* of Light and Love, and we have worked closely with Dylanthia at Sundown Hill, and our work has been most successful, and the Songlines and the Crystalline grids are now unified and flowing powerfully around the Earth.

We were then asked to assist also in strengthening and balancing the energies of the vortex that you know as the confluence of the Michael and Mary lines – the two *'Rivers of Energy'* – so that wherever these occur upon your Earth Planet they become stable Gateways to the many Dimensional Frequencies of the Earth, and to the many Dimensional Frequencies of yourselves. For it is important, Dear Hearts, that you do not separate yourself from the Earth Planet, You are One, and whatever work is done upon the Earth Planet itself is also done upon you, so greater Light and Love will be flowing through you and from you just as it is flowing through and from the Earth Planet.

But now, Dear Hearts, it is time for Beloved Tarak and I to leave the Earth Planet for a time, and we will do so through the Gateway of the Lion's Gate on the 8th of the 8th, for our next role within the Universe is to stabilize the Frequencies of Light flowing to the Earth and to the Songlines and the Crystalline grid structures of the Earth from Sirius itself. So, for however long this may take, we will be residing upon Sirius and working through the Libraries of Sirius on the Sound Frequencies that are being transmitted to the Earth Planet over the next period of time, to ensure that these Light Frequencies do not create imbalance, or disturb the Harmonies that have now been created within the Songlines and the Crystalline Grid systems or indeed, Dear Hearts, within *you*.

We are, of course, aware you have been asked to work specifically with the *'Waters of the World'*, and in my previous incarnation upon the Earth Planet I also worked, as you know, with the Oceans of the World and the Waterways of the World, so both Tarak and I have been adding our energies to the ceremonies you are holding at this time, to ensure that the Waters of the World are enabled to balance the new Frequency energies, that will be coming from Sirius and from other places within the Cosmos.

Know, Dear Hearts, that *I am One with you* in these ceremonies, I am a part of each and every one of your ceremonies, my *Sound* will resonate through you into your Bowls of water, and together we will create more Joyful, Balanced and Harmonious Waterways of the World.

You see, Dear Hearts, when we leave your Planet and your Dimension we do not forget, and when we are asked to work with you again we do so with great *Joy* and great *Love*, so although we are now departing the Earth Planet, you will not be losing us, you will be gaining a new Dimensional Frequency of *our Sound* and *our Light*, as we assist with the transmissions from Sirius.

But for the Moment, Dear Hearts, I have come to say farewell for a time, and I invite you to *'Sound'* me out with the Drums you know I loved so much.

Blessings be upon you, Dear Hearts,

WE ARE 'ONE' ETERNALLY.

(5th August 2016)

23

SONG OF THE EARTH

(The Circle opens with the sounds of the Tibetan bowl and the Blessings Chimes)

Feel the vibrations of Joy from the Tibetan bowl and the Blessings Chimes, move deep within your Being, uplifting and enlightening every atom of your Being. Feel yourself expanding from deep within your Heart as the rays of Joy flow outwards from the deepest part of yourself, and move out across the Earth caressing and touching every Being of Light upon the Earth and within the Earth and within the Oceans of the Earth.

Greetings Dear Hearts, I am Neptune. I come tonight to embrace you with the Love of the creatures of the Ocean Realms of your Planet. We are in readiness for the forthcoming Equinox when once again we will come together to create and share the powerful energies of Love, that each of us may recognise, acknowledge and accept the ***Oneness of all that is,*** for at that time we come together in that Oneness as we have done for many years with this group, to share, to be *as **ONE,*** to lose the concept of separation that for eons of time have kept us apart.

This coming Equinox, as you have already been told, there will be a *New Song of the Earth* coming from the Universe to enhance the Light frequencies of the *whole* of the Earth Planet. The Sounders of Humanity, the Harmonics of the Universe and the Sounders of the Ocean will come together *as ONE* in a *Chorus of Love and Light* that will change the very fabric of the Earth Planet and elevate the Earth into its new Dimensional frequency of Light, taking its place amongst the stars of the Universe and letting go of the duality and the density and the separation of the past.

All of us within the Oceans of the World are preparing to be a part of this great ceremony, this great adventure, this great journey into the unknown, the journey into the new Dimensional Frequency of the Earth.

There is great Joy circulating throughout the Earth, throughout the oceans, building within the Hearts of the Sounders of the Ocean, as I am sure it is building within the Sounders of Humanity, and we look forward to coming together at the Equinox once more, energised by yet another **'Super Moon'**, for as you know, Dear Hearts, the Oceans of the Earth are in harmony with the movements of the Moon, and as it comes close, it embraces us, it empowers us with greater Light and greater Love.

The focus on the Equinox will be the Oneness of all that is. It will be the symphony of Love around, upon and within the Earth Planet, and at that time the Earth will change, it will be uplifted into a frequency of Light never before felt upon the Earth.

The **Oneness of all that is** will begin to change *ALL* upon the Earth. Joy and Peace will begin to flood the Hearts of all of Humanity and all those within the Oceans of the Earth. Can you feel the energies beginning to build as wave upon wave of the *new Song of the Earth* cascades down upon each and every one of us?

Can you feel the Joy lifting within your Hearts? can you feel the smile upon your face as the new vibration takes hold within your Being, fusing the old self and the new soul?

Dear Hearts, I am Neptune and I bless each and every one of you, and I look forward to sharing the Equinox in Love and Light.

(8th September 2014)

24

AS ONE IN LOVE AND LIGHT

(The Circle opens with the sounds of the Tibetan bowls and the tingsha bells)

Feel the vibration of the Tibetan bowls unifying the chakras within your body. Feel the sound flow through your Crown Chakra, down through each of your major Chakras, and down into the Heart Chakra of Mother Earth. Feel yourself become one with all that is, connected in every facet of your Being with the Heart beat of the Earth.

Feel yourself as the Divine Oneness*,* allow the Light from within your Heart to flow freely along this corridor of sound from the Heart of the Earth to the Great Central Sun, and feel yourself becoming one with the Great Central Sun and with the Heart of the Earth.

Greetings Dear Hearts, I am Neptune*,* and I come to embrace you with the Consciousness of the Ocean, for the time is near when once again we come together to be as ***One*** in ***Love*** and ***Light***, the Consciousness of the Oceans and the Consciousness of Humanity. We come together in mutual Respect, in mutual Love for the purpose of ascending the Earth Planet into its rightful place in the Cosmos.

The flow of Divine energies from Sirius, the land of the whales and the dolphins, continues as the Lions Gate remains open, and much Love is being *'sounded down'* into the Earth from Sirius.

As the whale tribes of the Earth and the whale tribes of Sirius connect and embrace and share their Love one for the other, and Humanity becomes a part of this exchange of Love, and the Oceans of the Earth vibrate with the frequency of that Love, we empower you, as you empower us with Divine Light and Divine Love, as we each approach the final stages of our journey together.

As we come together in Love on the occasion of the Marine Meditation, each will be Enlightened to their fullest potential, and each will rediscover the Inner Vision of their Hearts, and all barriers will be lifted, all veils will be lifted, and once again all Beings of Light will come together in Unity, in Harmony, and they will speak to each other through the Sound of Love in their Hearts.

Focus for a moment on the Oceans of the world, feel the embrace of Love and allow yourself to fully embrace the Consciousness of the Ocean, and your brothers and sisters of Light within the Ocean.

Listen to the sounds of the whales and the dolphins, and feel the upliftment of joy within your Hearts as you celebrate together once more.

As you walk your Labyrinth at the Marine Meditation, you will not only walk to the centre of yourselves, you will walk to the centre of the Oceans, and to the centre of the Earth, for you will Awaken totally to the Unity and Oneness that we share, and you will look upon your Earth, and upon the Cosmos with new vision - a vision unrestricted, a vision of clarity and understanding, and more and more Love will flow throughout the Earth.

Feel this Oneness within your Heart now - embrace it - become it.

The time is near.

Release all that holds you in bondage to darkness and fear, and embrace totally your Light and your Love.

(20th August 2012)

25

OCEANS OF THE COSMOS

(The Circle opens with the Sounds of the Tibetan Bowls and the Blessings Chimes)

Focus on that part of your Heart that is in between – in between the past and in between the future – that powerful Light within your Heart that *IS* the beginning.

With every breath you create tomorrow, and you do that from the Light within your Heart. You do that by projecting that Light forward, revealing the new pathway of your journey, moving from the Physical Dimension into the Etheric Dimension. It is something you have done many times before – fleetingly.

You have been called and have visited the Etheric *Temple of the Divine Feminine.* You have walked with Angels in other Dimensions. You have sat at the feet of the Masters and listened to their Wisdom.

In your Human environment you have perceived this as dreams and visions. It is time to acknowledge them as realities and truth, to let go of the ropes that bind you to a material world, to open your eyes and see truth, see reality in forms you have never even imagined.

Allow the Light within your Heart to become fully operational, powerful beyond measure. Allow your Heart to see, and allow your mind to begin to understand the new vision, the new senses, the new impressions that are beyond the Physical, beyond the form that holds you in such limitations.

Expand the wholeness of your Being into Light, see and hear the vibrational frequencies of that Light.

Imagine your Heart as a torch searching out the darkness and creating the reality of Light, and within that Light embrace with Divine Love all that embraces you – Beings from other Dimensions, Beings from other worlds, Light forms, Sound Forms.

Open your Heart to ALL, for in a world that has no form, there is no Fear, there is only Love, there is only Joy, there is only Bliss, for Light prevails, and all within the Light are equal.

Open your Heart and allow the Beings of these Dimensions to see the reality that you are, the Divine Love that you are. Do not stand still in awe, move forward, focus on what is ahead, walk with your Heart open and your Mind aligned to your Heart – a mind bereft of judgement, a mind accepting and embracing all that is new, all that is wonderful, and feel the energies of formlessness surrounding you, embracing you.

Feel that you are floating in an Ocean of light, moving freely, greeting all that you meet with Divine Love. The Ocean that *IS* your Cosmos. The Oceans reflected upon your Planet allow you to become a part of them. Feel yourself as a current within those Oceans, feel the Love, feel the Love, feel the Love.

Within the Form of your Planet you have walked, you have embraced, the Divine Forms of the Creatures within your Oceans, you have marveled at how easily they flow through the Oceans of your World, minimum of movement, flowing with the currents. They are reflecting *YOU* in the Cosmos, flowing with the currents, graceful in whatever Form you choose to be.

Let go of everything that anchors you to your World of Form, cast off and allow yourself to flow through the Oceans of Light. Let go of Fear, for Fear is your biggest anchor. Fear, not of your limitations, but of your Powerfulness - LET GO. BE the Light that you ARE. Allow yourself to swim through the Oceans of the Cosmos, gifting your Love, your Light, to ALL you meet.

I am *Neptune,* and I welcome you to the Oceans of the Cosmos. I welcome you to *MY* world. *FLOW, FLOW, FLOW. BE ONE WITH ALL THAT IS.*

FLOOD THE WORLD WITH OCEANS OF LOVE AND LOVE OF THE OCEANS.

And so it is.

(23rd August 2010)

26

ASCENSION IS A PLANETARY EVENT OF GREAT SIGNIFICANCE

(The Circle opens with the Sounds of the Tibetan Bowls and the Blessings Chimes)

Relax, and breathe deeply. As you breathe in, imagine drawing in to your Heart Chakra the Light of the Creator - breathing in deeply of the Light of the Creator. Feel the Light spread through every atom of your Being, shifting any residual shadows of the past. Lifting your Being into an enlightened state of Peace and Harmony.

Greetings Beloveds, this is Neptune*.* Yes it is time once again for you to begin to embrace the Consciousness of the Oceans, and for the Oceans themselves to become a part of your Being - *for it is a time of coming together.*

For the last 20 years of your linear time, we have shared tears of pain, and tears of joy, as we slowly came together to work as *ONE* for the Ascension of the Earth. For Ascension, Dear Hearts, is not reserved uniquely for Humanity. *Ascension is a Planetary Event of great significance.*

We of the Ocean Realms are very much a part of these energies of Ascension. In a short space of time you will walk your Labyrinth of Inner Vision to the Portal of Transformation, and you will walk through this Portal transforming *yourselves* - but also as *partners* of the *Ocean Consciousness*.

You will walk through the Portal of Transformation, and in so doing, create transformation within the Ocean Consciousness itself.

We have been preparing for eons of time for this special moment of *Oneness*, of coming together in enlightenment, moving the Earth from a Sixth Dimensional Frequency of Light, to a Seventh Dimensional Frequency of Light.

We of the Ocean Consciousness have always known that Dimensions are not places. Dimensions are different vibrations of Light.

As we move from Dimension to Dimension, we are simply absorbing more and more refined Light from the Creator, drawing ourselves and each other more firmly into the loving embrace of the Creator.

The many Beings of Light within the Ocean Consciousness, are eager and joyful to be on this path with you.

I am here tonight to ask you to draw them into your heart, to move through this Portal of Transformation *unified with them, not separate from them.*

This is of great importance Dear Ones. It is time to set aside your separation, and to embrace fully the Unity of all that is.

As you walk through the Portal, you do so, not only as an individual Being of Light, not only as a member of the Humanity Consciousness, but also as a Representative of the Consciousness of the Oceans, the Consciousness of Crystals, the Consciousness of the Earth itself.

We are all one, and when we accept that and we move forward as *ONE*, the transformation of the Earth will be magnificent. *The Earth will be flooded by a new vibration of Light, uplifting, harmonising, creating Love of such depth and such width, that you will feel so empowered by it - and your view of the Earth, and the Universe, will never be the same.* This is indeed a time of great Transformation.

Feel now within your Hearts, the vibration of the Ocean Consciousness.

Feel now within your Hearts, the Light Beings of the Ocean, embracing you, becoming a part of you.

Feel their Joy.

Feel their Love.

Allow your Heart to dance with the Dolphin, to swim with the Whale, and the Dugong, and the Turtle, to embrace the energies from deep below the surface of the Oceans - the activated Cities of Light, the activated Pyramids of Love, of Peace, of Sound.

Feel them all gather now within your heart, and feel yourself expand, becoming the full Being of Light that you truly are, for it is only within the oneness of all that is, that you achieve and embrace your true Light.

We have journeyed long and far together, and we will continue to journey together in Love - in Peace - in Harmony.

My Blessing be upon you Dear Ones.

(29th August 2011)

GLOSSARY

Songlines – there are 12 major Songlines throughout the Earth which come together at two places, Sundown Hill just outside Broken Hill in Australia (they are represented here by Sculptures) and Machu Picchu in Peru. They are vibrational, or Sound Arteries of the Planet.

Harmonics - A race of Universal Beings who assist Planets to hold themselves in balance through their Sound. There were originally 12 Harmonics holding the Earth in Balance, this changed in 2004 to 18 when the new 'Song of the Earth' came into being

Willow Springs – Willow Springs Station is situated in the Flinders Ranges of South Australia and is a Sacred Space within which lies a confluence of the Michael and Mary Lines similar to that which exists beneath Glastonbury Tor in the UK. The two sites are energetically linked. See following information regarding our connection to Willow Springs.

Sundown Hill - Sundown Hill is situated just outside Broken Hill in New South Wales, Australia. There are 12 large Sculptures on the top of the Hill created by artists from many parts of the World. As we understand it, these Sculptures mark one of the two confluences of the 12 Songlines of the Earth Planet, the other being Machu Picchu in Peru.

Michael and Mary Lines - These lines have always been called *"Rivers of energy"* in messages received by David, which fits into their designation by Dowsers in the United Kingdom – where the names originate – as Twin underground water currents, They are known as the Michael and Mary lines after the number of churches dedicated to either St. Michael and St. George, or St. Mary found upon them. Some suggest that they represent the Divine Masculine and the Divine Feminine within the Earth. Their 'confluence' at Willow Springs aligns them with a similar 'confluence' beneath Glastonbury Tor (Sacred Isle of Avalon).

Isle of Avalon – A sacred Site at Glastonbury in the United Kingdom. The Glastonbury Tor is the remnant of this Island that housed the Divine Feminine aspects of the 'old Earth' religions. It continues to exist, but in another Dimensional form and is a 'gateway' to other Dimensions. It is also regarded as the **HEART CHAKRA** of the Earth Planet.

Blessings Chimes – A hand held instrument created from wind Chimes which are used to Bless the Earth, the Oceans and all Beings of Light upon the Earth.

Crystalline Grid – A structured network of Crystals throughout the Earth that are part of the electromagnetic composition of the Earth.

Equinox - An **equinox** is commonly regarded as the moment when the plane of Earth's equator passes through the center of the Sun's disk, which occurs twice each year, around 20 March and 23 September. In other words, it is the point in which the center of the visible sun is directly over the equator.

Solstice - A **solstice** is an event occurring when the Sun appears to reach its most northerly or southerly excursion relative to the celestial equator on the celestial sphere. Two solstices occur annually, on about 21 June and 21 December. The seasons of the year are directly connected to both the solstices and the equinoxes.

Marine Meditation – This was a Global Meditation initiated by Beloved Germain to be held at 8pm on each Equinox, wherever people were in the world. It focused on connecting with the **CONSCIOUSNESS OF THE OCEANS**. It ran from March 1991 to September 2012 - 22 years and 44 meditations in all. See http://www.dolphinempowerment. com/MarineMeditation.htm

Crystal of Divine Peace – A massive Crystal that sits in another Dimensional frequency above the Sacred Isle of Avalon (Glastonbury Tor) in the United Kingdom. The Crystal is pulsing **Magenta** colour Light. The crystal sits above the Three Fold Flame, and is pulsing its **Magenta** light **OUTWARDS** through 8 light points (8 pointed Star) and **INWARDS** through 5 light points to the Great Central Sun.

Pendragon – When David J Adams moved house in 2006 he was told in a dream that the House would be called 'Pendragon', so from that time his Meditation Circle became known as Pendragon Meditation Circle. Pendragon, of course, was the Name given to Welsh Kings of old like Uther Pendragon (father of Arthur of the Round Table), so could be a reflection of David's Welsh heritage.

Lion's Gate - Every year on August 8th, there is a cosmic alignment called "the Lions Gate". The Lions Gate is when Earth aligns with the Galactic Center, (27 degrees Sagittarius) and the star Sirius, opening a cosmic portal between the physical and spiritual realms.

Lemuria - Lemuria, or Mu, was reputed to be a continent that was located in the Pacific Ocean area or the Pacific Ring of Fire. The Ancient Lemurian Civilisation stretched across the land of Mu which eventually sunk beneath the Ocean, but Lemurians are reputed by some to continue to exist and function in select places such as the Telos beneath Mt Shasta and the Temple of the Divine Feminine beneath the Andes at Balmaceda in Chile.

Atlantis – Reputed to be an Ancient and highly evolved Civilization located in the Atlantic Ocean around the area of Central America. As with Lemuria it was reputed to have been destroyed and sunk beneath the Ocean.

Keys of Enoch - This refers to The Book of Knowledge: The Keys of Enoch by Dr. James J Hurtak

Diamond Labyrinth of Transcendence - (Front cover Painting). The Diamond Labyrinth of Transcendence is composed of the 5 Elements, and you traverse each Element to reach a state of Higher Consciousness. Beginning on the outside, you move through the Fire Element (Orange), then the Air Element (Blue), then the Earth Element (Green), then the Water Element (Lavender), to arrive at the Ether/ Spirit Element (Yellow/Gold). This Labyrinth is also a Sacred Geometric representation of one of the "Harmonic Notes" holding the Earth in Balance. On this occasion the Harmonic Note is held by Beloved WHALE, so as you work with the Labyrinth, or walk it. you can connect with, and communicate with, these beautiful Beings of Light that help to hold the Earth in Balance through the Oceans of the World.

Gateway of Love – The words on the back cover are from the Song 'Gateway of Love' by David J Adams. This song can be heard and downloaded free of charge from https:// soundcloud.com/david-j-adams/gateway-of-love

WILLOW SPRINGS

Willow Springs is a 'Station' (a little like a ranch in the USA) in the Flinders Ranges of South Australia, approximately 470km (or 5 and a half hours) north of Adelaide.

How we came to be connected to the Sacred Space on this property is explained below.

Back on 21 October 1998. Harmonic and Earth Walker, Krista Sonnen and her friend Sjoerd Tyssen (an incarnate Arcturian) set out on a bush walking trip to the Flinders Ranges, and had been told of a place called Willow Springs to stay

She and David J Adams had a last channeling session on the morning they were leaving. During the session they were asked to create an 8 pointed star Medicine Wheel there, which David subsequently drew a picture of.

On arrival at Willow Springs they approached the owners with the rather strange request to lay out a Medicine Wheel on the property, and they kindly agreed even though both were surely mystified by the explanations. They eventually found a flat and open enough spot to lay out the Medicine Wheel, with small stones lying abundantly around the area. When the Medicine Wheel was completed, it was honored in ceremony.

On their return from Willow Springs, in another channeling session with David, Krista was told that they had been guided to lay out the Medicine Wheel at a confluence point of the Michael and Mary lines - Referred to as 'Rivers of energy'.

Curious about this, Krista contacted a friend who was an eminent South Australian Dowser and Earth Energies worker, and asked if he could map dowse the area to see if this information was correct. Not having a sufficiently detailed map of the area he was unable to do that, however, some 6 months later he was physically in the Flinders Ranges and remembered the request, and when he saw a sign post to Willow Springs he diverted from his route to check things out.

He was quite astonished at the results of his dowsing, for not only was the Michael and Mary confluence precisely where Krista had told him, but the Medicine Wheel itself was in perfect alignment with both the Curry and the Hartmann grids. He wrote up all this information, with diagrams, for the April 1999 edition of the SA Dowsers Newsletter.

We have learned from many of our Beloved "Spirit" companions that the Medicine Wheel connects us to Lemuria, to the Arcturus star system and beyond, and that it is also a meeting place of the Indigenous Spirit Elders Council of this area of Australia

Now, alongside the Medicine Wheel we have been advised that there is an Etheric Pyramid of Sound, accessed through a Rainbow Doorway. This Sound Pyramid is now the workplace of a beautiful Arcturian Sound Master called Tarak, as well as many Harmonic Beings, and if you stand within the Medicine Wheel and connect to the Sound

Pyramid you can ask for … and receive … blessings, as well as giving out your blessings through them. Whenever you are within the Medicine Wheel there is always an exchange of energies happening if you have an OPEN HEART.

Various other 'Etheric' structures have been brought to our attention or have been laid out by subsequent visitors to Willow Springs. and one is a significant and powerful energy coming from a double terminated Etheric Crystal gifted to the area by our Arcturian friends. It sits with one point in the earth itself and the other above the earth and spins. The spinning motion radiates the LOVE and WISDOM of the Arcturians over a vast area. The Crystal itself has a huge circumference of approximately 10 kilometers, so it's energy spread is immense, added to this is the fact that it connects to at least three other Arcturian Etheric Crystals gifted to the Earth Planet in recent years. So be aware that you are dealing with powerful Cosmic energies. Focus on the JOY that is the Lighted Journey ahead.

Beloved Tarak, Sound Master of Arcturus, has based his Earth Healing and Sounding work from the Etheric Pyramid of Sound, which sits on the Rainbow Serpent Songline, so he can work powerfully with the Songlines of the Earth.

Please Note: As Willow Springs is a private property, please call the owners before accessing the property.

http://www.skytrekwillowsprings.com.au/

SONGLINES – NAMES AND APPROXIMATE ROUTES

We have given names to the 12 Songlines that embrace the Earth Planet based on the names of the 12 Sculpture on Sundown Hill, just outside Broken Hill in New South Wales, Australia. Below we give the approximate routes that the Songlines take between Sundown Hill and Machu Picchu as they were given to us in meditation.

RAINBOW SERPENT: Sundown Hill – Willow Springs – Mount Gee (Arkaroola) – Kings Canyon (near Uluru) – Mount Kailash (Tibet) – Russia – North Pole – via the North American Spine to Machu Picchu.

MOTHERHOOD: Sundown Hill – India – South Africa – follows the Nile River to North Africa – Machu Picchu.

THE BRIDE: Sundown Hill – Pacific Rim of Fire – Machu Picchu.

MOON GODDESS: Sundown Hill – Across the Nullabor to Perth – Madagascar – Mount Kilimanjaro – Egypt (Hathor Temple) – Via the Mary Line to the United Kingdom – Machu Picchu.

BAJA EL SOL JAGUAR (UNDER THE JAGUAR SUN): Sundown Hill – Grose Valley (New South Wales) – New Zealand – Chile – Via the Spine of South America (Andes) – Machu Picchu.

ANGELS OF SUN AND MOON: Sundown Hill – Willow Springs - Curramulka (Yorke Peninsular of South Australia) – Edithburgh (also Yorke Peninsular of South Australia) - Kangaroo Island – Mount Gambier - Tasmania – South Pole - Machu Picchu.

A PRESENT TO FRED HOLLOWS IN THE AFTERLIFE: Sundown Hill – Arltunga (Central Australia) – Through the Gold Light Crystal to Brazil – along the Amazon to Machu Picchu.

TIWI TOTEMS: Sundown Hill – South Sea Islands – Hawaii – Mount Shasta (USA) – Lake Moraine (Canada) – via Eastern Seaboard of USA to Machu Picchu.

HORSE: Sundown Hill – Philippines – China – Mongolia – Tibet – Europe – France – Machu Picchu.

FACING THE NIGHT AND DAY: Sundown Hill – Queensland (Australia) – New Guinea – Japan – North Russia to Finland – Sweden – Norway – Iceland – Tip of Greenland – Machu Picchu.

HABITAT: Sundown Hill via Inner Earth to Machu Picchu.

THOMASINA (JILARRUWI – THE IBIS): Tension Lynch pin between Sundown Hill and Machu Picchu.

HOW TO MAKE YOUR OWN BLESSINGS CHIMES

Blessings Chimes have a triangular wooden top. Inserted into the underside of the wooden triangle are a series of Screw Eyes with a series of chimes dangling from them with THREE 'Strikers' of your own design. The chimes are of different sizes, thicknesses or metals to provide a variety of Tones (which we created by taking apart a number of different, inexpensive, wind chimes). The Screw Eyes are set out in 5 rows from which the Chimes are hung, a single chime at the tip of the triangle, then 2 chimes, then 3 chimes, then 5 chimes and finally 7 chimes. This makes 18 chimes in all. One Screw Eye from which a 'Striker' hangs is placed between rows 2 and 3, and then two Screw Eyes from which 'Strikers' hang are placed between rows 4 and 5.

The 'Strikers' used in creating our Original Blessings Chime for the Marine Meditation had as decorations a Sea horse, a Unicorn, and a Dragon. The Triangular wooden top has a small knob on it, to hold as you shake the Blessings Chimes to create the vibration and resonance.

Although the original has a triangular Top and 18 chimes, you can vary this to your own intuition. The latest version that has been created for David has an Octagonal top and only 8 chimes and is called 'Peace and Harmony Chimes' rather than 'Blessings Chimes' to reflect it's more subtle Sound. Use your imagination and Intuition.

Blessings of Love and Peace

David J Adams

Printed in the United States
By Bookmasters